Oregon Trail Theology

The Frontier Millennial Christians Face
—And How We're Ready

Eric Atcheson

CHURCH
PUBLISHING
INCORPORATED

Unless otherwise noted, the Scripture quotations contained herein are from the Common English Bible, copyright © 2010 by the Common English Bible Committee. Used by permission. All rights reserved.

Book groups interested in study questions may find them on the book's web page at http://churchpublishing.org/oregontrailtheology.

Church Publishing
19 East 34th Street
New York, NY 10016
www.churchpublishing.org

Cover design by Paul Soupiset
Typeset by Rose Design

A record of this book is available from the Library of Congress.

ISBN-13: 978-1-64065-074-9 (pbk.)
ISBN-13: 978-1-64065-075-6 (ebook)

Printed in Canada

For my wife Carrie, whose love and compassion
remain the only home I will ever need.

For my women of valor: my mother Cheryl
and my sister Katherine.

For my father Gordon, whose moral compass burns brightly
within me to this day.

And always, as my Jesuit alma mater says,
for the greater glory of God. *Ad maiorem Dei gloriam*.

Contents

Acknowledgments

While writing often feels like a solitary endeavor, this book is simply not something that I could have completed alone. For inspiring and spurring me this far, my gratitude abounds for the following:

My editor at Church Publishing, Rev. Milton Brasher-Cunningham, for your patience with, and guidance for, a debut author. Our partnership is living proof that intergenerational collaboration is not only possible within the church, but that it remains exciting and full of possibilities. Both this book and I are far better for the care that you have invested in each of us.

My sea of friends and colleagues in professional ministry across the country and the world; like Legion, you are many, and like Legion's story, you proclaim a victorious Christ. Thanks to all of you, especially the minister for children and families at Longview First Christian Church, Jamie Lynn Craig, for your friendship and ministry. Keep on building the kingdom.

My ecclesiastical superior, the regional minister and president of the Northwest region of the Christian Church (Disciples of Christ), Rev. Sandy Messick. For your guiding and mentoring of this pastor—and many, many others—in their calls under your charge, I remain very grateful.

Those authors whose writing has genuinely changed my life—most of all Rev. Carol Howard Merritt. In a world rife with ego and envy, you have offered me nothing but holy encouragement.

My friends whom I only see on Twitter and Facebook—you truly are a community for me. The authenticity, passion, and humor you exhibit in our conversations and commiserations alike are always among the highlights of my days and weeks.

The congregations that welcomed me in and set me on a right path as a student associate minister and a seminarian: First Christian Church in Concord, California, and their then-pastor,

Rev. Dr. Russ Peterman (now of University Christian Church in Fort Worth, Texas); and Tapestry Ministries in Berkeley, California, and their ministry team.

The church that called me to serve as their pastor for six-and-a-half years: First Christian Church in Longview, Washington. Thank you for taking a leap of faith on a fresh-out-of-seminary cleric to be your minister. I miss you all, and you remain in my prayers just as I hope I remain in yours. Additionally, portions of this book were written while on a sabbatical leave from First Christian Church, and that sabbatical is a gift for which I will remain forever grateful.

My alma maters that built upon the religious education that my Disciples of Christ tradition began: Lewis & Clark College in Portland, Oregon; the Pacific School of Religion and Graduate Theological Union in Berkeley, California; and Seattle University's School of Theology and Ministry. I am likewise grateful for their financial generosity, and that of the Disciples Seminary Foundation in Claremont, California, for making my education possible.

Lastly—and most of all—I give thanks to my family, who never stopped encouraging me with their love to answer the call of God ringing in my ears. To my in-laws, Bill and Nancy Hamby—I am glad you don't mind that I told a story about you here!—thank you for welcoming me into your family as your daughter's beloved. To my cousin, Hagop Mouradian—your chronicling of our family's story that I convey in part in these pages is a blessing. I hope that our ancestors are proud of us both as we continue testifying to what they survived so that we might one day live. To my uncle, David Atcheson, and my parents, Cheryl Pilate and Gordon Atcheson—your authorial and lawyerly feedback on my manuscript drafts and my contract legalese alike were invaluable. Thank you for that—and Mom and Dad, for everything you've done, always. To my sister, Katherine Atcheson—grasshopper, I could never want, or ever imagine having, any other sister. And finally, to my wife, Carrie Atcheson—you are my lifegiver and my light in every way imaginable. I am so very grateful every waking day that God saw fit to make me yours.

Why Take This Journey?

"I was never so contented and happy before."
"I long for the quiet of home where I can be at peace once more."
"I had never found a place to call my own."
"I did not think I would feel comfortable until I came here."

The first and second of these four sentiments are from the letters and diaries of two young pioneer women—Narcissa Whitman and Agnes Stewart—who were twenty-eight and twenty-one, respectively, when they each wrote those words during their sojourns along the westward Oregon Trail.[1] The third and fourth are simply refrains that I have heard time and again, in slightly varying forms, from friends, peers, and congregants concerning the institutional American church.

I have come to believe that the refrains never really change, only the century in which they are uttered. The lack of belonging, the need for something new, the continual search for what so many of us crave and what not nearly enough of us ever really find—all of those motivations swirl in the mixture of purpose and desire that we religious types tend to refer to as a calling.

I genuinely believe that many of the pioneers who traversed their way across the continent in covered wagons during the mid-1800s did so out of a sense of calling. Many also did so out of a sense of greed for the land itself, and for the homes of the American

---

1. "Narcissa Whitman," National Park Service, *https://www.nps.gov/oreg/learn/historyculture/history2.htm*, last updated February 24, 2015, last accessed December 11, 2017; and "Historic Trail Quotes," Jim's Trail Resources, *https://jimstrailresources.wordpress.com/trail-quotes/#historic-trails*, last accessed December 11, 2017.

Indian peoples[2] who inhabited it. But many a family dared to pick up the only life they had, pack up or sell all they owned, and take a life-or-death gamble on the chance that they would survive the six-month journey from Missouri to Oregon, and the subsequent settling down in a new home that they had never before seen.

I likewise genuinely believe that the millennial generation traverses its way across the spiritual landscape—from church to church to no church and perhaps back to church again—out of much that same sense of calling. Broadly speaking, millennials are our young people who were born between the early 1980s and the late 1990s, and many of us were raised on a series of 1990s-era cultural staples, such as Nicktoons, R.L. Stine's *Goosebumps* series, and, of course, the *Oregon Trail* video game franchise. Many of us retain nostalgia for these icons of our childhood, but it is the last one, the *Oregon Trail* franchise, that has stuck to us so much that older millennials are even sometimes referred to as the Oregon Trail generation. And when it comes to describing our spirituality, I find it to be an apt label.

For even as we see others working within the church out of a sense of Prosperity Gospel-driven greed or politically minded self-ishness, many a millennial has dared to pick themselves up on Sunday morning and take a gamble on a chance that they would not only feel included in the church they were visiting that day, but that they would thrive there. Though the headlines blare that my generation is the most godless ever, the most likely to shun organized religion ever, and—according to that iconic opening clip of Aaron Sorkin's hit television show *The Newsroom*—simply the worst ever, I know in my heart that I belong to a generation that, far from being godless or hateful of church, is instead a generation crying out

---

2. Occasionally in this book, you will see me refer to the indigenous tribes of the Americas as "American Indians." I utilize the names of specific tribes whenever possible, but I also want to acknowledge and honor the fact that there exists no consensus opinion on the preferred term for the indigenous tribes of the Americas. I have elected to use the term "American Indians" here in deference to the dissatisfaction expressed by some American Indian leaders and activists towards terms such as "Native American."

from thirst. Even as we are inundated with twenty-four-hour news cycles, two-day Amazon Prime delivery, and dating apps for every demographic imaginable (find your soulmate on Left-Handed-Postmodern-Christian-Pastors-Mingle.Com today!), we crave the depth of those relationships that we have chosen rather than those based solely on who our family is or what job we perform. Friendships of truly great depth are forged in the fires of social media, Reddit, and online forums. We fan ourselves when a favorite musician or athlete likes one of our tweets. We plan entire road trips to meet in person friends whom we know only from the internet. We find recognition, affirmation, and community in new places as they emerge.

None of this may seem to have a lick in common with the far more primitive world of the intrepid pioneers of the 1800s, yet I promise that it does. For, faced with the prospect of wilting away in lives that were less than what they could be, those pioneers left the circumstances in which they found themselves. In like manner, we millennials, having long since realized that our parents' and grandparents' churches were not always going to nurture us out of wilting, have sought to strike our own paths.

Just as the pioneers of old loaded up their wagons with what they needed—staples, clothing, hunting arms, and ammunition—so too do we load our lives up with what we spiritually need—podcasts, new books, social media, and much more. Far from merely being glued to such digital temptations, millennials have found liberation in them; our spiritual fixes can now come on Monday through Saturday, not just Sunday morning. They come in the briefest of fleeting moments and in hours upon hours of conversation. They come from far outside the church's walls and, yes, sometimes within them too.

So why take this journey? Because we are a generation unbounded, for better and for worse. And I wouldn't have it any other way. We take it upon ourselves to journey outward because it is fundamentally a part of who we are, and it is a journey that we are ready to take.

I sit here typing these words in my childhood home in the suburbs of Kansas City, not very far at all from where the pioneers pushed off on their journey across the United States. Kansas City will always be home to me, and it is a fitting setting to spring off when talking about a new generation's travels and travails alike, and for myself especially: after graduating from high school nearly thirteen years ago, I moved to Portland, Oregon, for college and have remained on the "Left Coast" ever since. Whether in the north of the Willamette Valley like the pioneers, or in the Bay Area like the forty-niners of the San Francisco gold rush, I have lived and learned new lessons to build upon the strong Midwestern roots that Kansas City gave to me, and my gratitude for those roots abounds.

As a traveling pilgrim, I continue to carry gratitude not only for what my home has given me, but for what the church has given me: to be a provider of truth, goodness, and meaning where there previously had been a lack of such virtues. My hope for the church is that it can still inhabit such roles in the lives of my generation, even though it will require a great deal of work and self-examination. My desire and prayer for you, dear reader, is that the following chapters will provide you a bit of the truth and goodness that I know my generation seeks, and still yearns to find, not just within the institutional church, but outside of it as well.

The frontier this generation faces is the fundamental reshaping of that institutional church which, in all honesty, has been decades in the making, and certainly longer than either I or the *Oregon Trail* video game have been alive. Yet a combination of sociological, theological, and economic factors have converged to create this present spiritual frontier.

Just as I have, this book will follow the Oregon Trail, from starting off in Independence, Missouri, to traveling the trail, to, God willing, arriving home. There is a lot of trail to cover. It begins with an inventory of the baggage my generation brings with us to the church gates and how we are still capable of joyfully surrendering that baggage to the love of a community in which we can fit. It ends with a forceful critique of the state of American Christian spirituality in an era of a resurgent white Christian nationalism. I hope you will find comfort and challenge alike in what humble testimony I can offer you in these pages.

The first two chapters of this book focus primarily on illustrating the circumstances at hand. You may have read some of the myriad think pieces in newspapers and magazines about how we millennials are vicious, unstoppable serial killers of all manner of treasured cultural artifacts. I think it is important to offer an explicitly spiritual interpretation of my generation.

In chapter three, we will begin to pivot away from the wider circumstances of the present and home in on how millennials, and spiritually inclined millennials in particular (including Christians), have adapted to those wider circumstances in our ordering of priorities, finances, and other critical aspects of our lives that in turn can inform our spirituality.

Chapters four through seven outline those adaptations in specific areas of millennial spirituality and community-building, and then describe how they can be used to great effect: how we form online connections and friendships, how we heal from emotional and religious wounds, how we lead from a place informed by our understanding of God, and how we engage in the politics of the Trump presidency and all of its attendant prejudices and newly enabled enmities.

That is an awful lot to try to cram into one book, and I do not expect you to see this work as the definitive treatment of such an important and pressing concern to both the church and the rising millennial generation. But it does seek to describe at some length the journey that we are undertaking together, and I am eager to take the trail with you, regardless of your generation. We are all in this wagon train together.

To my elders, the Greatest Generation and the baby boomers and perhaps even some of the older Generation X-ers: please do not take my championing of my generation as a personal slight upon yours. If ministering in two intergenerational congregations over the past decade has taught me anything, it is that on this trail of faith that we blaze together, the wagons in our trains need not be circled up and segregated by age. Indeed, I have learned much as a child at your knee and now as a young adult. I would not be the God-image I am without you.

And to my fellow young people: I pray my words here will put a song in your heart and a fire in your spirit. You surely put a song and a fire in mine.

Finally, to those even younger who come after me: my deepest desire for you is that you will be as passionate for your causes of justice and peace, whatever they may be, as I know that my generation is for ours. I will be saying a prayer of thanksgiving and encouragement for you.

Overland Park, Kansas
December 2017

Chapter 1

Matt's General Store
What We Bring with Us

My eyes cast over our refinancing options. I see a lot of numbers with commas separating them every third number. Even though we are talking about buying a house in addition to refinancing my wife's medical school debt, I am not accustomed to computing household budgetary matters that have that many zeroes, especially on the negative side of the ledger.

The surprise and dismay on my face must register to my wife, because she pipes in helpfully, "Look, I know you're not familiar with just how expensive medical school really is. I've been living with these student loans for years now. I'm used to it. I know you're not. But you'll get there."

You could skate across the look I give over my eyeglasses and the papers in my hands. Despite her words of reassurance, I am not convinced. Between student loans, a car loan, and a potential mortgage, I am terrified that we are going to have to auction off the naming rights for our firstborn child just to keep the lights on.

Appealing to our shared goofy sense of humor, my wife tries again. "This amount of student debt is like a big, smelly walrus that I've just gotten accustomed to living with. I call him Clyde. Clyde's smelliness is just now hitting you. But you'll get used to living with his stink too. And when all our debt is paid off, we will throw a huge 'Clyde is dead!' party."

A loud guffaw escapes from my previously clenched jaws, momentarily easing my worries—and startling our two dogs, Sir Henry and

*Dame Frida. But with student and car loans plus the mortgage on the
house that we are about to buy, the amount of money we owe seems a
more suitable figure for describing the national debt.*

*We are not alone in that regard when it comes to our generation.
Our finances are no longer just a statement of values; they are a statement of inhibitions and obstacles as well.*

As the American Church faces down an existential and financial crisis on a par with the economic collapse that brought about the Great
Recession that my generation faced as we completed college, many
of the young families and households that are seen as highly valuable in church planting and recruitment literature are facing similar
financial crises, but on a more microcosmic scale. We lack assets.
Cash is spent as quickly as it is brought in. In order to maintain any
semblance of a quality of life, or to attempt any real furthering of
our circumstances in life, we often must take on substantial debt.

One would think, then, given the financial similarities between
so many churches and so many millennial-aged households, that
the former would have a more apparent understanding of the latter,
even if begrudgingly so. After all, we millennials may be the generation of fidget spinners, smartphones, and avocado toast, but we also
have a deep and abiding need to make a difference in our world, just
as churches feel called to build the realm of God where they are. In
spite of the financial chains which hamper millennials, we remain
determined to make an impact. Jacques Berlinerblau, a professor at
Georgetown University, says of us:

> My [students'] career plans are a peculiar mix of naked ambition
> and hair-shirt altruism. If they pursue investment banking, they
> do so not merely to make money. Rather, they wish to use their
> eventual wealth to distribute solar light bulbs to every resident
> of a developing nation. They'll apply to the finest law schools in
> hopes of someday judging war criminals at the Hague.[1]

---

1. Jacques Berlinerblau, *Campus Confidential: How College Works, or Doesn't, for Professors,
Parents, and Students* (New York: Melville House, 2017), 187.

Ideally, those needs—or callings—would have intersected more than they have so far in the emergence of millennials as fully formed adults. Yet they have not. Between 2010 and 2015, the percentage of millennials who said that the church has a positive effect on the way things are going in the United States today plummeted from 73 percent to 55 percent.[2] The reasons for this precipitous drop in my generation's approval of the church are manifold, and as an increasingly homogenous church looks down on increasingly diverse generations of young people, I would be surprised if that figure were not already lower.

The antipathy towards the church from younger generations is real, and in many cases reciprocated. Yet many millennials have resolutely remained within the realm of spirituality, hoping, praying, and striving to change it from within rather than taking our cards and going home. We millennial Christians have not given up on the body of Christ, and we are determined to find our own communities within it, even if it means migrating away from the brick-and-mortar communities in which we were raised and that our elders keep impressing upon us are our sacred duty to save.

In order to both explore and affirm that perseverance of my generation, I want to turn to another name by which we are sometimes called: the Oregon Trail Generation, a term that was coined in 2015 by entrepreneur Anna Garvey.[3] It serves as a moniker more precisely applied to the older millennials (in addition to some very young Generation X-ers) who were raised on a steady diet of MECC's *Oregon Trail* video game series in which players led a fictitious covered wagon party to Oregon. *Oregon Trail* as a game and a cultural phenomenon has so deeply penetrated our pop culture that video parodies, card games, and "You have died of dysentery"

---

2. Hannah Fingerhut, "Millennials' Views of News Media, Religious Organizations Grow More Negative," *Pew Research Center, http://www.pewresearch.org/fact-tank/2016/01/04/millennials-views-of-news-media-religious-organizations-grow-more-negative/*, January 4, 2016, last accessed December 11, 2017.

3. Anna Garvey, "The Oregon Trail Generation: Life Before and After Mainstream Tech," *Social Media Week, https://socialmediaweek.org/blog/2015/04/oregon-trail-generation/*, April 21, 2015, last accessed December 11, 2017.

memes have all been byproducts of the original game's massive pop-
ularity. In other words, *Oregon Trail* is something whose presence
eclipses more than just one generation, or one subset of a generation, and is instead a more widely, if not universally, understood and
shared phenomenon.

It is precisely because we millennials—and younger Gen
X-ers—played so much *Oregon Trail* that it is useful in describing
our generation's sojourn through faith. From beginning the trail
after already being loaded up with so much baggage that we need
a team of half a dozen oxen just to make some forward progress, to
having to bargain our way through the grief and consternation of
things breaking down and going wrong, the mechanics of *Oregon
Trail* gameplay offer an apt springboard to not only explore how
millennials have come to live out their faith, but to celebrate it,
affirm it, and offer ways to dive deeper into it as well. Let us begin,
then, with an honest look at how many of us have begun these adult
journeys of the soul.

How We Got Here

In the original *Oregon Trail* games, you could choose not only your
occupation, but the riches with which you began the game. You
could choose to be a farmer from Illinois with a very small savings
account, a carpenter from Ohio with savings double that of the
farmer, or a banker from Boston who was absolutely loaded. The
object of the choice was to inject a variable degree of difficulty into
the game. If you were a beginner, you could choose to be the banker
with vast reserves of cash, and if you wanted a challenge, you could
elect to be the cash-poor farmer.

Whatever your occupation, you began the trail itself at the same
place: Matt's General Store in Independence, Missouri, where you had
to outfit your wagon party with oxen, sets of clothes, spare parts, food,
and boxes of bullets. Matt would helpfully chime in with advice, but
beyond buying at least a yoke of oxen to slowly haul you off to Oregon, you could purchase as much or as little as you wanted—or that

you could afford. If you did not buy all you could at Matt's General Store, prices got progressively—and prohibitively—more expensive along the trail. It was the economy that we millennials walked into after college, but written into a computer game decades beforehand: limited cash to invest in our livelihood at the start, which has meant paying a higher and higher price as time has elapsed. Starting conditions were, and are, everything.

I graduated from college a scant eight months after the collapse of the investment firm Bear Stearns set off the Great Recession. I already knew that I would be going to graduate school—seminary—for at least three more years, so I had somewhere to wait out the immediate devastating effects of the crash. However, as I would quickly learn, the market was still suffering in the spring of 2011, when I earned my master of divinity in May, was ordained in June, and began my first day at my new church in Longview, Washington, in September. I was profoundly fortunate, though. I had classmates who waited years for their first calls out of seminary. My friends in other fields, from law to teaching to healthcare, for which they had invested vast sums into their education, likewise suffered. They went months, even years, either unemployed or underemployed as jobs were eliminated via attrition and older employees delayed their hard-earned retirements because of the deleterious effect the recession had on their retirement investments.

All of these factors, as well as many others, also affected congregations through decreased giving, and congregations were forced to quickly adapt to such scarcity. There was one church that interviewed me for an associate pastor position. On paper, it looked healthy and was looking to expand its staff. But at the interview, they admitted that they could only guarantee the position for a two-year period; after that, its existence would largely depend on whether congregational giving had begun to improve.

For some millennials, the variability and mobility that comes from changing jobs may be welcome, even sought after, especially since so many of us cannot even afford mortgages, much less are looking for one that would tie us to a particular city or town for several years. But as we will see in chapter three, the leaps of faith that millennials have taken in response to such variability aren't always for a job. And for other millennials, especially those emerging from expensive degree programs with hefty debts to repay, a relatively low-paying job that may not be around in a year or two has the potential to become a real obstacle, not a help, to paying the bills—especially if it is a job we relocate for.

Now, take such a socioeconomic circumstance and throw into the mix a congregation that is continually preaching tithing. Theologically, there is nothing wrong with the practice of tithing. I do it myself as a pastor because in part, as my seminary field education supervisor told me, "Never ask your congregation to do something that you are not willing to do yourself." But I am also a part of a two-income household that is essentially fiscally solvent despite juggling the debt of student loans, car loans, and a mortgage. Such solvency has become a luxury rather than a necessity for our up-and-coming generations. When you have student loans to pay off and car payments to make, there is often precious little left for tithing to a church, much less any charitable giving at all. What little giving can be done, ironically, sometimes goes towards the GoFundMe campaigns[4] of our friends and relatives who, faced with unexpected expenses of their own, are forced to ask their loved ones for cash to repair their financial breaches. Setting up a GoFundMe may be seen as more respectable than panhandling because it does not take place on a street corner, but the circumstances that necessitate it are sometimes no less dire or dramatic, precisely because there is so little opportunity to create any sort of safety net in our unforgiving economy that has yet to bear the occupational fruit that was promised. That lack of forgiveness extends to church, where millennials are often seen as takers rather than as givers in part because of our relative lack of financial security.

---

4. For anyone who is unfamiliar, GoFundMe is one of several "crowdfunding" websites that offer the service of helping a person raise money for anything, from a business start-up to medical bills, in exchange for a commission on all the monies raised. Because donations often come from peers rather than wealthier donors, crowdfunding can result in people without vast reserves to draw upon redistributing their meager funds amongst each other.

Preoccupied with Our Occupation

What we do for a living, and how we make ends meet, remains a foundational source of identity in American culture. Think of how many times you meet someone new and, perhaps without even thinking about it, ask them, "What do you do?" As much as millennials are made out to be artistic and sensitive snowflakes in perpetual search of safe spaces to create whatever their art happens to be, the jobs that have opened up for our generation frequently do not allow for such creative expression unless we force the issue. Having been raised on an educational curriculum that emphasized the creation of one's own voice not only in the traditional venues like English class, speech, and the debate team, but also in a bevy of extracurricular activities, millennials have come of age in a world that wants us to continue being children, or even pets: to be seen and not heard; to simply be grateful for the crumbs that fall to us from the adults' table.

Think of the Syrophoenician woman in Mark 7 who begs Jesus to heal her stricken daughter. After Jesus cuts her down with the withering comment, "It isn't right to take the children's bread and toss it to the dogs," she maintains her dignity and responds, "Lord, even the dogs under the table eat the children's crumbs."

I have seen many pastors and writers assuage their discomfort with what is pretty clearly an ethnic slur from an Israelite towards a Syrophoenician by saying that Jesus was satirizing such attitudes, but there is no indication in the text of mirth or parody on his part, just as there is no indication that she took Jesus's comment in jest. It seems accurate—albeit ghastly—to view Jesus's comment, then, not as some joking commentary but as an insult.

Here is where Jesus returns to the role of teacher, role model, and, indeed, Messiah. Having conceded the rightness of the woman's response by saying, "Good answer," he assures her that her daughter has been healed. The woman's response to Jesus makes it clear that she is not content with the crumbs that fall from the adults' table; she wants to be treated as an equal at that table. Jesus, in turn, grants to her the miracle that she was seeking. Her daughter is made well.

Millennials realize that the dignity that comes from our occupations is innately valuable. We do not demand economic or financial miracles. We have been conditioned to accept our position beneath the table, and the pitiful few crumbs that fall our way, as though some kind, benevolent soul at the table were surreptitiously slipping us sustenance the way I "accidentally" drop scraps on the kitchen floor for my own dogs. Being endlessly reminded that "the world does not owe you a living" is among the least nutritious of those crumbs, and one that is typically reserved for us. But if that line of reasoning is an inadequate word of comfort to an older manufacturing worker whose job has been outsourced despite their skill and dedication, then why is it of value to someone younger than that worker?

Younger generations are not stupid. That sounds self-evident to the point of being borderline ludicrous, but I will double down on it because of how urgently it needs to be said: Younger. Generations. Are. Not. Stupid. We know when we are being talked down to, we know how to recognize doublespeak and passive-aggressive mockery, and we know that if we are to make a living off of our passions we must find people, companies, and entrepreneurs who are willing to pay us to pursue those passions.

As the cultural landscape has dramatically changed over the past ten to fifteen years with the arrival of social media and digital apps, new needs have emerged, and for those of us whose passion involves meeting those needs, there is no better time to be alive. Those occupations may not be the same as being a farmer, or a carpenter, or a banker, but what they offer us is not all that much different than what the Oregon Trail offered its own wayfarers: a chance to start something new out of the sheer will to bring about a new thing, whatever it might be.

New Economies Necessitate New Communities

If I could communicate one of the most basic truths that I believe informs the actions of both the historical Oregon Trail generation and the modern-day Oregon Trail generation, it is this: new economies necessitate new communities. The United States of the

1840s and 1850s had not quite reached the apex of the Industrial Revolution, but its primarily agrarian (and, in much of the country, slavery-driven) economy had already begun to permanently morph, and the industrial capacities of the Union played a significant role in its eventual victory over the Confederacy. Similarly, today in the early twenty-first century, the Digital Revolution is in full swing, and much of the economy that has been in place since the Industrial Revolution has lamentably been outsourced, shuttered, or outright demolished. Some of the biggest brands of the twentieth century, like Pan American and Sears Roebuck, have given way to newer upstarts that have become titans in their own right, like Southwest and Amazon. They, in turn, may well cede their titan status someday, if for no other reason than such the nature of the proverbial economic beast.

Changing consumer preferences have had a lot to do with the demise of many storied brands, but where those changing preferences come from is not simply a matter of a proclivity for dating apps and eschewing chain restaurants. The changing economic preferences of millennial adults have emerged in what has thus far been an intractably stunted earning potential relative to older generations, to the tune of a nearly 20 percent loss in earnings relative to the baby boomer generation when they were our age.[5] Our economy is, at its core, one of increased scarcity. It is a tidal change to which we are still adapting, both economically and spiritually.

When we transverse the bridge between economic and spiritual realities, how much of our church life has remained unchanged since the twentieth century? I do not mean the fundamentals, like the study of scripture or the Sabbath worship of God or the administration of a church, but more how we go about those fundamentals. We still preach and teach the sacrificial giving of tithes and offerings to our spiritual communities—that has never and hopefully will never change—but is the only avenue for doing so at your church the Sunday morning collection plate, or does your congregation also enable online or

---

5. "Millennials Earn 20% Less Than Boomers Did at Same Stage of Life," *Associated Press*, *https://www.usatoday.com/story/money/2017/01/13/millennials-falling-behind-boomer-parents/96530338/*, January 13, 2017, last accessed December 11, 2017.

mobile-based gifts with a credit card or an e-commerce service? We still proclaim the value of Bible study—something else that will hopefully never change—but is the only Bible study class at your congregation offered at a time that is convenient for only one generation?

I cannot stress the premise of that last question enough. This book is not a manifesto for a millennial-run monopoly on the church. Rather, it is a plea for a millennial-aided church, a church that has made space sufficient enough and sacred enough for millennials to be able to flex our spiritual and moral muscles. These muscles are strong indeed, even when they have propelled us away from the church. In fact, it is often because of the strength of those muscles that our departures have taken place. This strength of moral resolve on the part of my generation has led to a mass exodus that has unfortunately become far too familiar as more and more millennials recognize the toxicity of some, or much, of what we were once taught.

An Exodus of Conscience

I grew up in the Christian faith, attending both a Catholic and [an] evangelical church. Despite the theological distance between the two, one thing remained: homosexuality was a sin. They didn't even talk about trans or genderqueer folk because it was all the same to them.

I entered college with shards of faith still clinging on, one element of which was the oft-spouted "hate the sin, love the sinner." It didn't take long to realize that telling someone their existence is sinful translated as abhorrent regardless of whether one believes [and] had nothing to do with compassion.

That revelation was my first big step towards coming out as an atheist. I'm still so ashamed I thought that way for even a second about the truly beautiful, talented, and loving queer folk in my life.

These words from my longtime friend Lauren cut through me like a sharply honed blade when I saw them. Despite our disparate religious worldviews, we have maintained a solid friendship for a number of years after squaring off against one another many a time on the collegiate debate circuit. Intellectually curious and passionate for a more just world, Lauren is raising her young daughter to choose her own religious path, whatever it may be, including the possibility that her daughter's own path might diverge significantly from her own at some point in the future. It is one of the things that I appreciate most about her. She is raising her child to be her own person, and not a carbon copy of the original article, no matter how good a person the original article may be.

But reading Lauren's testimony of leaving the church, I found it impossible to begrudge her reasons. I grieved the church's loss of such a soul, but even more strongly, I realized that I had to grieve that the church has inflicted such losses upon itself with countless other Laurens. Their exodus—largely driven not by laziness or malice, but by conscience—is a reckoning that we cannot blame them for. The church is responsible for our decades of not engaging the spiritual concerns of an entire generation.

Is the church truly loving our neighbors—our immigrant neighbor, our LGBTQ neighbor, our addicted neighbor—rather than simply saying that we do? Is the church really being salt for the earth and a light for the world as Jesus demands of us in the Sermon on the Mount? And has the church truly integrated this generation into its fold, or has it shunned its young off to the side, like a subdepartment seen as a particularly undesirable assignment within a sprawling conglomerate?

When the church marginalizes a generation, that generation picks up on what is being communicated: You. Do. Not. Belong. Here. Millennial Christians, and the Generation Z Christians who are, to my great joy, fast rising with the gospel behind us, are not oblivious to the signals being sent. It is not that we have not heard the message of the church; on the contrary, we have heard the message loud and clear, and have consciously reacted by stepping back.

A critical part of American Christian spirituality in the twenty-first century, whether or not we wish it were so, is having to acknowledge, understand, and empathize with the grievances and complaints of those who have been leaving the church over the past couple of decades. It may not be the job that we had hoped for, but to simply say, "It is not my job" is to completely miss the heart of the stories in the Gospels that depict Jesus acknowledging, understanding, and empathizing with those who initially disagreed with his teachings. In Mark 10, a rich young man approaches Jesus and asks what he must do to inherit eternal life. Upon hearing this man's question, the Gospel says, Jesus looked at him and *loved him*. And the rich young man's subsequent walking away did not end Christ's love for him.[6]

What I struggle with in this story is that I see in the rich young man not just my generation's deep-seated need for spiritual righteousness, but also the older generations' prioritization of possessions over experiences. The rich young man's foregoing of a lifetime of discipleship under Jesus in favor of his possessions resonates with every time I have seen a church prioritize its own possessions, be they pews or hymnals or even the buildings themselves, over its kingdom-centered mission according to the Great Commission: to go and make disciples. Just as the young rich man was focused only on himself, many churches have elected to focus on their own pet issues rather than on what Jesus calls the "more important matters of the Law" in Matthew 23:23: justice, peace, and faith.

So, is the church really prepared to love a generation that has been told repeatedly that those who have spent decades championing cultural wedge issues over justice, peace, and faith do not give a whit about what the young think about those pet wedge issues? If so, the church must do a far better job of it. If not, it is high time to own that unwillingness, lest its duplicity implicate the church even further in the pushing aside of a potential generation of Jesus followers.

A Desire for Life, Not Death

In spite of such experiences at the hands of the institutional church, I believe that many millennials, even atheist millennials, do not

---

6. The rich young man is by no means a one-person band on the list of those who initially disagreed with Jesus's teachings but were still left moved by him. Think of the Samaritan woman at the well in John 4, or Simon the Pharisee in Luke 7, and consider how they, unlike the rich young man, were able to see past their personal preferences and understand what Jesus was asking of them.

necessarily want to see the church die off entirely. Lauren is not raising her daughter to be an atheist. She is raising her daughter to pick
a path all her own that may well include a profession of faith in God
someday. That is not the mark of a hardened heart; quite the contrary, it is the fruit of a heart of openness.

Despite that openness—from both millennials and the churches
and pastors who claim to want to minister to us—there remains a
massive cultural chasm between millennials and the church that I
believe remains traversable. As much as there are characteristics of
my generation that separate us from previous generations, there are
also a great deal in which we remain like our forebearers. Even when
it comes to characteristics that are often regarded as quintessentially
millennial—like access to technology and the repetitive news cycle of
information that is increasingly equal parts disruptive and addictive—
we surprisingly share in the experiences of our elders. In such matters,
it seems, misery—or at least consternation—loves company.

According to the Christian research firm Barna, 54 percent of
adults struggle with the onslaught of information from the twenty-
four-hour news cycle. Despite the stereotype of our being much
more in love with our smartphones, 56 percent of millennials do
as well.[7] Among baby boomers, 44 percent report that they would
struggle to go an entire day without internet access, as do 47 percent
of millennials.[8] Even when it comes to issues closely associated with
our generation, our concerns often align with those of other generations, and theirs with ours. I can attest to this from personal experience. As much as social media has shaped the millennial experience
of relational ministry, it is often my social media friends whom I
have never met in person, many of whom are Gen X-ers or baby
boomers, who frequently voice the same concerns as mine on any
number of issues, from politics to popular culture. Indeed, they are
often able to get me to think about such things in ways that I otherwise might not have, and that means the world.

7. Jun Young and David Kinnaman, *Hyperlinked Life: Live with Wisdom in an Age of Infor-mation Overload* (Grand Rapids: Zondervan, 2014), 25.

8. Ibid, 60.

On a more spiritual note, while it is true that many millennials are divorcing themselves from organized religious trappings at a rate greater than their elders, we in fact show similar levels of spiritual practice compared to older generations when they were at the same age as millennials. Research indicates that millennials engage in prayer at almost identical rates to those of Gen X-ers when the latter were coming of age in the late 1990s, and at only slightly lower rates than those of the baby boomers during the early 1980s (which is the earliest statistical data available for the baby boomers).[9]

So, let us be clear as we discuss how we got here, and what baggage we are carrying at this point in the trail: there are differences between generations, sometimes vast ones, but in other ways, our values and our concerns are quite similar. Instead of a gaping void between the generations of the church, imagine a canyon: it winds along, with some areas where the gulf between each cliff seems intractably large, and others where the sides are so close that it feels as though you could reach out and touch the other.

Instead of feeling threatened by an impending millennial coup that may or may not ever happen (once we have had our fair-trade, organic, shade-grown, handpicked-by-the-Vestal-Virgins coffee and logged onto our Slack thread, we will let you know if the coup is still a go), let us recognize the smaller gaps that can be bridged, those shared concerns and values, and let us utilize them to facilitate a peaceful passing of the baton from one generation being in power to another.

More to the point, we must arrive at some sort of power-sharing arrangement. The sheer length of the boomer and silent generations' reigns of power, in both the church and the government, has shut out not only millennials, but Generation X-ers as well, even as the eldest among their ranks are already transitioning into their mid-fifties. The United States just replaced its only president born after 1946 with its third president born *in* 1946, risking a gap not unlike the twenty-two-year canyon between the birth year of George H.W. Bush and the

9. Paul Taylor and Scott Keeter, eds., "Millennials: A Portrait of Generation Next," *Pew Research Center, http://assets.pewresearch.org/wp-content/uploads/sites/3/2010/10/millennials -confident-connected-open-to-change.pdf,* February 2010, last accessed December 20, 2017, 93.

birth year of Bill Clinton, George W. Bush, and Donald Trump. An entire generation was shut out of the American presidency. We risk doing the same thing again. Instead of fearing a generational coup, can there instead be openness to having a few more sets of younger hands on the levers of power? I continue to hope that openness remains possible, in spite of the church's tendencies to the contrary.

Washington Post columnist Dana Milbank tried to explain why the baby boomer generation insists on keeping its power, writing as a part of his own lament on behalf of his Generation X compatriots: "Boomers, coddled in their youth, grew up selfish and unyielding. When they got power, they created polarization and gridlock from both sides. Though Vietnam War–protesting boomers got the attention, their peers on the right were just as ideological, creating the religious right."[10] The themes of being coddled in their youth and growing up selfish should sound familiar: they parallel in striking detail many of the critiques made today of millennials.

We will talk more in chapter seven about how the historical context of the Religious Right has been a contributing factor in turning millennial Christians away from the institutional church, but suffice it to say for now that Milbank's indictment, scathing though it is, gives voice to many of the grievances of not just the Gen-Xers but also the millennials. Milbank refers to his generation as the "clean-up crew" for the baby boomers, but at what point does that generational sharing of power take place—and not just in the halls of government, but in the pews at church? What might such a power-sharing arrangement even look like?

The Problem of Denial

So much ink and emotion have been spilled over the imperative acknowledgment that the institutional church must change or die that it is hardly necessary for me to belabor the point here. Rather, a

---

10. Dana Milbank, "Baby Boomers Have Been a Disaster For America, And Trump Is Their Biggest Mistake Yet," *Washington Post*, https://www.washingtonpost.com/opinions/2016 / 10/25/7d0c6a62-9aef-11e6-b3c9-f662adaa0048_story.html?utm_term=.aab28ae6fd7a, October 25, 2016, last accessed December 15, 2017.

fundamental postulation to make going forward is that one crucial piece of baggage we carry with us, one obstacle that continues to bedevil the legacy church, is one of Elisabeth Kübler-Ross's stages of grief: denial.

A prerequisite to envisioning a church in which millennials are not shut out of its life and mission is a basic acknowledgment that the church itself has never ceased breathing, living, and changing into something new throughout its entire history. Yet so much of church life is spent mourning what once was, or what might have been. The churches of the mid-twentieth century, with their teeming classrooms of children and their packed pews each Sunday, are wonderful for a church to strive for once again, if that is truly the vision. But to strive for it by trying to replicate the churches of the 1950s by means of the methods of the 2010s and 2020s is where, I think, the church has begun to lose a bit of perspective. The attempt to reproduce a bygone era is where our mourning of the past becomes worship of the past, which constitutes a form of idolatry. Too often, the church is using its gifts and resources to worship an idealized, revisionist vision of the past, leaving the future church on the outside looking in, because that vision of the past will never be ours.

Those are perhaps harsh words to hear about any congregation's outlook and institutional memory, in part because denial is very good at blunting such truths. Yet what the church must follow is Jesus Christ, not a particular decade's or era's way of discipleship.

The expectations we take with us on this trail of spiritual transformation and understanding of Christianity can make all the difference between a connection with God as revealed by the Church of Jesus Christ and further spiritual disenchantment. It is entirely possible to have that connection with God without membership in a congregation, but community has capacities that enhance this divine connection in ways that solitude does not. But to eschew the chance to deepen this attachment to God through community is precisely what many souls have done. That millennials are foregoing church involvement on a week-to-week or even a month-to-month basis is hardly news, but we are eschewing the church even on special occasions. For instance, there has been a 37 percent decline in weddings taking place at religious institutions since 2009.[11] Not coincidentally, the timeframe of 2009 to the present intersects with both the dramatic aftereffects of the Great Recession and millennials beginning to come of age and getting married.

Given the economic realities detailed thus far, being asked to help foot the bill for years' worth of deferred maintenance on church buildings does not rank highly enough for many millennials. For us, being the church has to do more with what it can do now, not with what it once was, because we were not around for those golden-era years.

I have to think that any organization in any other field would react quickly to such shifts in interest and relevancy, and yet, a whopping 61 percent of people report that they gained no new insights about God or their faith the last time they attended church.[12] It is a near-perfect statistical summation of the church's collective denial: people see the church as irrelevant, and are treating it as less important not only in their day-to-day lives, but for special occasions as well. Despite much hand-wringing and existential angst over the future of American Christianity, the church appears not to be bothered enough to offer the people who do show up anything new to say.

If the church cannot acknowledge that millennials continue to face a uniquely bitter-tasting brew of economic circumstances the likes of which we have not seen since the Great Depression; and that those circumstances have, along with the dictates of our consciences, necessitated a departure from practicing Christianity as our forebearers have done for decades and centuries; and that in spite of it all, we still remain very much attached and attuned to the notion that there is indeed a God who created us and loves us—then, yes, it will be a difficult ask for the church to adapt to this new frontier.

---

11. "Cost of US Weddings Reaches New High as Couples Spend More Per Guest to Create an Unforgettable Experience, According to The Knot 2016 Real Weddings Survey," *The Knot, https://xogroupinc.com/press-releases/theknot2016realweddings_costofweddingsus/*, February 2, 2017, last accessed December 15, 2017.

12. "Americans Divided on the Importance of Church," Barna Group, *https://www.barna .com/research/americans-divided-on-the-importance-of-church/*, March 24, 2014, last accessed December 15, 2017.

Denial, however, will be a difficult stance for the church to maintain. Pretending that things have not changed and that the church can continue as it always has, catering to the same programs and systems that are increasingly unsustainable simply because we have forgotten what the church was like without them will be more painful in the long run. The church has always been changing, growing and evolving organically over time. The more we try to approach it as a de facto time capsule surrounded by a world that is organically changing and growing, the more we risk doing real and lasting harm to the realm of God that we are called to help build in this life.

If the church's fear of change and growth is greater than our fear of dying, then we are listening more to denial than to the hope, which is simply no way to faithfully be the church. If it were, millennials would be right to keep on walking toward the exit rows, because the message would be that the current church fears millennials, and what they have to offer, more than the church fears death. Considering Christians worship a Savior who taught us that death can indeed be overcome, a Savior whose resurrection compelled Paul to write in 1 Corinthians 15, "Where is your victory, Death? Where is your sting, Death?" then the Church must embrace the organic growth of the body of that selfsame Savior instead of steadfastly and stubbornly accepting the death to which its spiritual paralysis sentences it.

What This Book Is Not

Having described the conversation I hope to have with you throughout these pages, and the scope of the task that sits before a generation and the church that simultaneously chases after it and pushes it away, it is prudent to take a moment to discuss what this book is not. Broad, sweeping, or universal claims are best left, I think, for the most basic of truths about God as a God of love for all people. This book goes well beyond such foundational claims about the nature of both God and the church. It is far sounder, then, to reserve my words here for what may be thought of as both my generation's and the church's respective general directions, while also recognizing that there is more than one set of directions to get from one point to another, or that one could simply forego attempting to arrive at that point at all. Quite simply, generalization is not the same as universality, and claiming the latter is not my aim.

While I am using research data to draw certain conclusions about millennials and the church, particularly within the United States, these conclusions will be largely about the trends and directions I see in my generation's complicated relationship with Christianity. Considering how wonderfully diverse both an entire generation and the entire church are, these identifications of trends and waypoints are not meant to be seen as universally applicable claims, but as observations of the direction in which many millennial Christians are currently traveling.

Put a different way, I would never dare to be so bold as to call this the definitive work on the millennial generation's relationship with the church. Other worthy treatments have already been created, and I am sure even more will be written in the years to come. Mine is one voice of many adding to the conversation currently taking place in the public square alongside valuable perspectives from other writers, pastors, poets, and thinkers. Far from settling the matter, I hope what I offer will further spur those conversations already taking place, add another layer or dimension to them, and offer new affirmation to millennials who would, in spite of everything, dare to follow Jesus, and in so doing change the world.

I will be drawing extensively on my own personal experience as a pastor alongside my citations of research data, both because I am a storyteller by nature and by vocation, and because I have come to believe that the relatively impersonal nature of data and statistics can benefit from the personalization of one's narratives, stories, and memories. This project, then, strives to embrace both. Without the data, I would not be able to place my personal journey into its wider context of the journeys of many other millennial believers. Likewise, without the stories, I would not be able to do justice to the impact of the data.

A substantial influence of many of those stories—of my story—is the positive impact that my elders, the Gen X-ers and the baby

boomers and the silent generation, have had on me. This book is not
a polemic by one generation against another. It is a compendium of
stories, considerations, and reflections that seeks to affirm and celebrate how one generation—the millennials—has come to understand
and practice Christian spirituality, while also telling other generations
of how and why our practice and understanding of Christianity has
come to be. Our practice and understanding of our faith should not
be taken as a threat, even though in my experience it often is, both
because it is something new in an institution that positively venerates
tradition, and because it is still being formed.

One final thing this book is not is a eulogy for the church. The
conclusion that Christianity, and especially institutional Christianity,
is doomed in the United States, or in the occidental world as a whole,
cites some of the same statistical evidence cited here. It already fills
plenty of books and articles. Even if that were my perspective, I would
have scarcely little to add to those tomes. Nor is this book a diatribe
of why the church is dying and how millennials are the ones who are
burying it. Those books and articles, too, have all been written already.

Rather, I request that you think of this book as a possible rededication of and for the church. In my denomination, the Christian Church (Disciples of Christ), infant baptism is usually practiced
only in cases of extreme emergency, as our preference is to wait for
the newborn to reach adolescence before they make the conscious
decision to follow the Way of Jesus Christ. Infants, then, are dedicated rather than baptized (think of the opening scene of Disney's
The Lion King, where Rafiki anoints Simba and hoists him aloft).
A child who comes into our tradition having already been baptized
as a baby is often asked to affirm that previous baptism and rededi-
cate themselves to the profession of faith in God as revealed by Jesus
Christ that baptism represents to us.

The fundamental question this book asks is: can the church be
rededicated to following the Way of Jesus Christ instead of adhering to a single generation's methods and practices of following the
Way of Jesus Christ? Asking the church to follow Jesus sounds so
simple, even insultingly simple, but even in Jesus's experience, often

the simplest of requests can be the hardest to fulfill, such as those of Luke 6:37: do not judge; do not condemn; forgive, and you will be forgiven. We do so much of the first two and so little of the third.

It is the same with our rededication to and of the church. To love and follow God, and to love each other, sound like exceedingly simple requests for Jesus to ask of us, but they have proven exceptionally arduous for us to live out, so much so that we struggle and wrestle every day to do what is right by God and by each other. Our rededication must involve an acknowledgment of so many truths that the church has been slow and often recalcitrant to admit: that we must be better at honoring and adjusting to the needs of others, that we need to be putting those needs ahead of ours a whole lot more often, and that far too frequently, we repurpose the programs and missions of the church to serve our own selfishness rather than God and the world.

All of these tendencies of the church have had a role to play in arriving at the reality of a generation that wants the least to do with organized Christianity of any generation in recent memory. This is how we got here. We chose to stock up on goods that ended up poisoning the spiritual diet for so many young people that they simply quit the community as a result, a decision far easier to arrive at today than on the historical Oregon Trail, where a decision to leave a wagon train was often a one of life and death.

There are indeed life and death implications at work today as well, not just for the spiritual lives of the people who are leaving, but also for the wagon train of the church itself. We can acknowledge that reality and seek to change how we govern ourselves out on the trail, or we can continue along our wagon-wheel-made ruts of denial, and hope we still make it to Oregon regardless.

But if the church were to listen to what God may be saying to it through this new generation and consider a change of course, courageous and difficult though that may be, I can at least promise that the church will not end. Both the world and the church will be better off for the Church having shown the courage to embrace a change of this magnitude as not only possible, but also Spirit-led.

Chapter 2

Leaving Independence
The Joyful Surrender of Community

I was sitting in the crowded fellowship hall, enthusiastically absorbing the lecture being presented by a role model—and now friend—in ministry, Carol Howard Merritt. She led the assembled group of (mostly) clergy through an exercise. Beginning with the eldest members of the audience, and then slowly moving on to the younger attendees decade by decade, she asked us to share aloud with the assembly what the formative moments of our childhood were, both for us personally and for the generation to which we belong.

Most of the events named were occasions that one would likely expect, the sort of watershed moments that we were taught about in our history classes. The end of the Second World War. The assassination of President John F. Kennedy. President Richard Nixon's resignation. The Oklahoma City bombing. September 11, 2001. The sort of life-changing occurrences so colossal in their effects that we remember exactly where we were when we first heard the news.

After spending a few minutes on each decade, Carol arrived at the final decade of births—those of us born in the 1980s (I should note that this event took place a few years ago, a time when I, born in 1986, was among the youngest in almost any gathering of clergy). She asked us the same question she had put to those who came before us. Only a couple of us were able to offer up our responses—the World Trade Center and Pentagon attacks of September 11, 2001, and the global financial collapse of 2007–08—before several of our older colleagues began jumping in with how those events affected them compared to the other events they had named, in ways that surreptitiously questioned the ways my generational peers had said these seismic events had formed them. I watched one generation talk over another, in a crowded venue, in real time.

I sat there silently, a scowling, stewing heap of a self-righteous, indignant millennial (if only there were fidget spinners back then—I would have been a living cliché). These are colleagues I looked up to— and still do. But I am not sure that they had any idea what they were doing in that moment, and that what they were doing is exactly what the church has done for years: assert the primacy of their narrative in response to alternative stories that vary from theirs.

Years later, I reflected upon this memory with Carol. Her response to me communicated volumes. "It happened almost every time I did that exercise," she said.

We often choose to bowl alone, play solitaire, and fly solo when it comes to our own lifelong quests of spiritual enrichment and religious fulfillment. Much as I appreciate the richness of such solitude as an incorrigible introvert, I still steadfastly believe that it is within the context of communities that do good, rather than harm, that we are able to truly get the most out of our quests.

Harm, however, can be a relative thing. There are the nightmare stories of congregations throwing conniptions over the "irreparable harm" that would be caused by the choice of color for the new hymnal covers, or the new location of the adult Sunday school room. But those reactions (a) trivialize the very real emotional, spiritual, and financial harm that churches have historically been capable of inflicting, and (b) are apt to break open chasms through which even more people drop out of the beloved community, perhaps never to return.

It is that latter impact which necessitates an honest dialogue about what the surrender to a community of Christ should look like. While the church may publicly say that it wants this dialogue, the inhospitable welcome it offers to younger generations is not conducive towards such surrender.

Surrender is a bit of an "insider" term in American Christianity, so permit me a moment to define it for our purposes. Surrender, in this context, involves a conscious letting go of the desire to have your personal preferences catered to. Having your wants and desires come first is fine when it is your birthday party, or the day you become a Nobel laureate or an Academy Award winner, but much less so when it is in the context of church built around the ministry of a Messiah who famously taught that the first shall be last, and the last shall be first.

Such a surrender is not merely an outsider going to church for the first time on a Sunday morning, then perhaps a second, and a third, and then deciding to brave the church membership class and be promptly signed up for a small group or a weekly Bible study. Surrender must also be a conscious and deliberate act of the group who welcomes the outsider. The group doing the welcoming must surrender some of their assumptions about what God may be doing in and through this newfound community member. In church, unlike in war, the act of surrender must be reciprocal.

Reconsider, then, the story of my well-intentioned, but ultimately inwardly looking colleagues. They had been in ministry for longer—and for some, much longer—than me. They had fought the good fight, as Paul would say; they had run the race. Many of them are still running that race with all of the same passion as before. But, when given an opportunity to hear what their younger colleagues had to say, and to surrender the power to wholly shape the narrative which was being built collectively, they ultimately and loudly declined.

Here is the challenge of surrender the church faces: to hear not only our own voices, but to actively refocus our attention on the voices of the newcomers to the assembled group. It is a challenge that I hope and pray that the entire church can rise to with grace and humility.

Greenhorns and Trail Leaders

Independence is an appropriately ironic name for a town that served as the launching point for the pioneers who had gathered from across the country to have a go at surviving the trail to Oregon. In order to make it to Oregon, where they could live in a state of relative independence, they had to bind themselves to the rules and social mores of a wagon train that might consist of anywhere from a few dozen to literally hundreds of people—a small town in its own right. It goes to show that as much as Western culture tends to celebrate the notion of individual independence as a supreme state of being, we have to surrender some of our individual claims if we are to ever live in harmony.

In the earliest of the *Oregon Trail* games, your rank at the end of the game, which was determined by your final score, reflected the hierarchies of the wagon trains: you could end up a rank-and-file greenhorn, who would have had no additional say in the governance of the wagon train; or an adventurer; or a trail leader, someone elected or hired to lead the wagon trains, and who had significant social and political power. In retrospect, it may not have been such a bad thing for the game to assign such titles at the end, rather than at the beginning, because few of us take well to a drastic demotion—myself included. Privileges and status, once granted, are very difficult to sacrifice.

Yet any position, and its attendant privileges, will eventually be forfeited. We pass away, move away, step aside, or sometimes just slowly drift away from the day-to-day trappings of our responsibilities. The handoff of stature and power in society and the church alike is as inevitable as death and taxes. Rather than embrace that inevitability as something that ultimately frees us from our burdens after a job well done, when God can say to us, "Well done, good and faithful servant," we attach onerous conditions to the performance of that job for those who might come after us. Those conditions, in turn, make it difficult to find people to perform such tasks. If we are honest with ourselves, that may sometimes be the aim of such conditions. Such a way of doing things tends to exist not to accomplish important tasks, but to hinder such accomplishments, by maintaining a status quo that advantages those with positions of power and influence.

Too Many Chefs, Too Few Millennials

When I began as a factory-fresh pastor in Longview, I was quickly overwhelmed by the sheer dimensions of the job of full-time ministry. The spiritual and emotional stakes, the history of my venerable congregation, and even the size of the parish's board of directors all proved to be daunting to a minister who still had his "Made in Seminary" tags attached.

The structure of our board of directors at the time was a representational one, by which I mean that it was required in the church bylaws that almost every demographic in the church be represented, even if there was no other functional need for that representation. The elders, deacons, women's ministry, and Sunday school, among others, were required to be represented at board meetings. It was an onerous obligation for a small congregation, and it made the board an unwieldy instrument of governance. We had too many chefs preparing the broth. Our decisions had an overabundance of decision-makers.

When congregations take notice of this dynamic, their remedy is often a solidification of the roles for the same decision-makers, meaning their power structures become more, rather than less, centralized. In contrast, our approach in Longview entailed a full year of discernment to see how our bylaws might be changed to facilitate a more productive means of governing ourselves. I picked the brains of colleagues who had led their churches through similar changes, I revisited my seminary textbooks on different governance structures within congregations, and we prayed and deliberated together as a community.

At the end of that year, we presented an amended set of bylaws to the congregation for open discussion and a vote. The criteria of board membership as a representation of individual ministries was

jettisoned because it had led to burnout and feelings of not ministering in capacities most suited for some of our hardworking members'
God-given gifts. We replaced the representation requirement with
a task-performing criterion, in which board members were chosen
based on their willingness and ability to either perform specific tasks
or serve in a flexible, at-large capacity.

The results were immediate and noticeable. Board meetings
were both shorter and more productive. We addressed agenda items
more quickly and responsively. The board itself became a group of
people who worked extremely well together and continued to do so
even as new officers were elected to replace many of the ones who
had selflessly helped usher in this change. Burnout of our volunteers
became less of an immediate concern.

Particularly meaningful to me was that we began to see millennials serving as board members, elders, and deacons. Under the previous structure, there was little space for our millennials, who were
faithful Jesus followers but floated outside of the constituencies that
were explicitly assigned representation in our bylaws—our elders,
deacons, and so on. Those traditional constituencies can be very
important but have often proved not to be the best way of integrat-
ing younger churchgoers into the ebb and flow of congregational
life. Freeing ourselves of the requirement of membership in another
group to sit on the board meant that we began to see millennials in
positions of substantive leadership and in front of the church as a
part of worship, and I rejoiced in witnessing that change.

Part of the change involved significant surrender of *de jure*
power on the part of those who had sat on the board in the old representational capacities. But far from kicking up a fuss about it, they
embraced the change and gave our new board members the space
to do the work of the parish well. It was a sublimely Christian act
of surrender for which I continue to be grateful, because it changed
our humble community for the better. Nobody pretended as though
their preferences were more important than our family of faith, and
we were far the richer for it, because it nudged us outside of our
established comfort zones.

What if, on a more wide-reaching scale, the church did not see the surrender of power and status as a threat to the Most-Holy-And-Sacred-Way-That-We-Have-Always-Done-Things, but rather, as an opportunity to live out that annoying gospel value Jesus taught about leadership by sacrifice? Can we see the spiritual richness in acts of denying our own self-status on behalf of Christ's church? Can our trail leaders accept living in church as greenhorns, and allow former greenhorns to take the reins as trail leaders? And might there be a way forward for the church in which all generations can be heard? Can we create space to hear every voice, and not just the voices of a select few?

I believe there is such a way, one that takes us from our worship of independence to our embrace of interdependence.

From Independence to Interdependence

There are many phrases I wish I could ban from church, were it in my power to do so—which is why it is a good thing that I do not have that particular power—but here is a partial list:

- The word "just" when praying. ("God, we just pray because we just need you, just . . .")
- "Love the sinner, hate the sin." (How charitable of you to still love a screwup like me!)
- "God helps those who help themselves." (No, God absolutely does not, just ask Job.)

But the phrase at the top of my list has to be "a personal relationship with Jesus Christ." It drives me utterly bonkers for several reasons. The phrase is not found anywhere in the Bible. It takes something beautiful and communal—Christianity—and makes it "all about me." And it takes the existence of Jesus Christ as a Messiah not only for the Israelites but also the Samaritans, the Syrophoenicians, the Canaanites, and even the Romans who killed him, and sacrifices it upon the altar of Western individualism. It makes our affinity for

Jesus—and Jesus's affinity for us—entirely inward, at least where soul-sized matters of redemption and salvation are concerned. We become independent Christian entities, rather than the one universal catholic (small 'c') church proclaimed in the Apostles' Creed.

That is, in a nutshell, the church of independence. It is not to be confused with Independence, the small town outside of Kansas City where the Oregon Trail began, and where wagon trains set off together. It is a church of independence from full community in Christ, and as such, is akin to the many go-it-alone, "spiritual-but-not-religious" practices of many in the millennial generation. The church of independence has emphasized over and over again to us millennials that our relationship with the divine is entirely personal in nature. And eventually, we wised up to the fact that so personal and inward a relationship with God hardly required membership in a church and its attendant cultural rigidity and inflexibility towards outsiders.

The church of *interdependence*, in contrast, recognizes that revelation of the divine remains firmly within the realm of community, to the extent that weighty matters of the soul like redemption and salvation must be spoken of in communal terms. The church of interdependence recognizes that people must not be sacrificed upon the altar of doctrinal purity, and that without other people to share in the joy of the Holy Spirit, such doctrinal purity is ultimately useless. Even if the church stumbled upon some great revelation of divine truth, that revelation's impact is severely limited if we are unable to communicate it in the most effective and inclusive of ways.

Emphasizing only the "personal" relationship with Jesus Christ as necessary for salvation often pushes younger seekers away due to its inherent inflexibility. Instead, the church could move from seeing each believer as wholly independent to seeing each person as a unique entity within a larger spiritual community. For while the church may claim to live out Paul's "one body, many parts" illustration from 1 Corinthians 12, the truth is that the church often sees those parts as independent, not interdependent.

The tendency to value independence over interdependence becomes relevant when considering the present church's own interdependence

upon its future incarnation in the form of the people outside the
church who may one day opt in, and those who have not yet been
born into the church but someday will be. That future church will be
an incarnation of immigrants in every sense of the term: souls who
are not yet at the place where they will eventually arrive. That defini-
tion of immigrant may even include you. And that is by design.

A Country of Immigrants—and a Congregation of Immigrants

Almost every time another xenophobic policy or proposal gets
dropped by the current administration, from the border wall
to the travel ban to the rescinding of Deferred Action for Childhood Arrivals (DACA), I see the same hashtags resurrect themselves on Twitter: #WeAreAllImmigrants. #NationOfImmigrants.
#ImmigrantsWelcome.

I used to utilize some of these hashtags myself, though I no longer
do because I realize that we are not entirely a nation of immigrants.
The American Indian peoples did not immigrate here as my ancestors did, and the ancestors of my African- and Caribbean-American
siblings were kidnapped and shipped here in chains to be sold into
chattel slavery.

Still, it is a maxim that is commonly recognized enough to
merit a couple of questions: Why view only our country as a community of immigrants? Why not also view our congregations as congregations of immigrants? Yes, many (perhaps most) congregations
have members who have attended since birth, but I would be willing to bet that most Christians are currently members of congregations other than the ones in which they were raised. They may have
grown up in a different church, a different denomination or faith
tradition, or they may not have been raised in any faith tradition at
all, and were led by the Holy Spirit to find the one faith family that
they have ever had.

The gold standard we tend to hold for evangelism efforts is to
reach "unchurched" people, or the "lost," or whatever label we—often

patronizingly—use for people who are unaffiliated with any organized religious community. The debate that often follows within the church is how to best integrate the newcomers into the congregation (which, in this context, is often simply a euphemism for "assimilate"), with much less discussion and deliberation about how the congregation can integrate itself into the lives of their new souls.

The conversation often goes something like, "They are members now; did we assign them to a small group? Check. Can we tell them that the nursery/youth group/mission team/et cetera is always looking for new volunteers? Check. If they do well there, how soon can we think about asking them to serve on the board/diaconate/elders/vestry?" The dialogue is concerned with subsuming the new faces into the existing infrastructure of the congregation without asking whether God has placed them there to bring about something new and wondrous to behold instead.

Those of us who, years ago, joined a religious community other than the one we were birthed into have perhaps forgotten what it was like to be the immigrant, to be the stranger in a strange land who did not know that the chancel had to be arranged just so for Pentecost Sunday, and that the second, not the third, Sunday of every month was casserole day for the fellowship meal.

There is nothing innately wrong about traditions. They give weight and meaning to the community that abides by them. They enable connections between one another, and between us and God, to be built and strengthened. Yet often in church life, the tendency seems to be for the job of casserole-cooker or paraments-arranger to become a tradition that must be filled at all costs, even if the need for that job has lessened or even disappeared.

What if, instead of filling pre-existing positions, we in the church move, much like immigrants, to where we see work that needs to be done? What if we begin to see ourselves as migrant workers and begin to honor our own rootlessness a bit more, and thus increase our valuation of actual immigrants in ways that do not involve building walls or demanding that certain languages be spoken? After all, as the Hebrew Bible states, God's people were once immigrants in the land of Egypt, and their collective memory of that experience informed certain ethical and moral responsibilities afterwards.

You Were Immigrants in the Land of Egypt

*Any immigrant who lives with you must be treated as if they were one of your citizens. You must love them as yourself, because you were immigrants in the land of Egypt; I am the L*ord *your God.*

—*Leviticus 19:34*

Sandwiched in between Leviticus 18:11 and 20:13—two of the "clobber" verses some Christians have used to bully LGBTQ people—lies a rich trove of ethical and theological guidance in Leviticus 19, from which Jesus draws one of the two most important commandments that he cites in Matthew 22: to love your neighbor as yourself (Leviticus 19:18). It is where farmers are instructed to leave behind a portion of their harvests for the poor, an exhortation that any of us, whether we are farmers or not, can take to set aside some of the fruits of our own labors for the poor and the outcast.

It is also where we find the command, in Leviticus 19:34, to treat and love the immigrant among us as we ourselves would want to be treated and loved. One verse earlier, we are likewise exhorted to treat the immigrant among us with fairness, and to not cheat them.

The context is not immediately translatable—the Israelites were enslaved in Egypt—but the sentiment is: we are not meant to forget what it feels like to be the outcast, the outsider, and the stranger. You were immigrants in the land of Egypt, says the verse. The command comes, then, not as a theory or a hypothetical, but on the basis of personal experience, a collective memory not unlike the collective memory we see elsewhere in the scriptures, like the citations in the New Testament of the exile in Babylon, even though that exile took place some six hundred to seven hundred years prior to the New Testament's composition. This particular collective memory does not belong to Christians—the enslavement in Egypt belongs to Jewish tradition—but we are called to take its lessons to heart because of its place in our sacred scriptures.

This lesson of drawing from personal experience has another side to the coin: if we are incapable of drawing empathy for others based on our personal experiences, then we must listen to the experiences of others and let them teach us. The slowness with which churches have proven willing to listen and learn from the experiences of millennials is one of the reasons churches have largely lost us. Consider the story with which I opened this chapter about my well-intentioned colleagues talking over the millennial pastors in that workshop. That experience is hardly an isolated one; I frequently vent with my colleagues in ministry who are also my age peers about our shared frustrations with not being taken seriously within both our congregations and our denominations. After being told that we are the future of the church, we have come to realize that, in many ways, the church is not fully prepared to listen to that future, even as we stand in front of the congregation, pleading to be heard.

Petri Dishes of Toxic Homogeneity

There are times when I do not think church has socially evolved much higher than the high schoolers in the 2004 film *Mean Girls*. The movie came out as I was moving from high school on to college, and it resonated both with me and with a generation of older millennials in its depiction of just how capriciously insular teenagers can be to one another, even at the expense of their own humanity. But the cliquish behavior depicted in *Mean Girls* is hardly limited to our schools. At churches, people stake out the exact same seats in the sanctuary and fellowship hall, going so far as to tell an unsuspecting newcomer that they are sitting in "their" seat, as though seats could be reserved in a church like they are at a stadium or on an airplane. It always saddens me when I worship somewhere over multiple Sundays and see people sit down for the post-worship coffee hour at the exact same tables, while the visitors that day end up eating completely alone. It makes church feel like we are only a hop, skip, and a jump away from announcing that, like the junior plastics in *Mean Girls*, we wear pink on Wednesdays.

Though such cliquish behavior is both timeless and ubiquitous, there is more to it than that. The power imbalance that continues to persist within congregations and denominations ensconces small-minded cliquishness into systemic ways in which outsiders are shut out from the parish's culture, power structure, and opportunities. What begins as a *Mean Girls*–type scenario where the church insists on their Wednesdays in pink can be indicative of a toxic culture lurking beneath the surface, as this anecdote from a Presbyterian pastor and blogger, Derrick L. Weston, points towards:

> Every effort I made to think through ways of inviting new youth into the church or to develop programming for young people was met with either indifference or outright hostility. To make it worse, the loyal young people we did have in the church were treated very poorly. They were critiqued for what they wore to church. Their behavior when they stayed in worship was analyzed. They were looked down upon when they didn't stay in worship. It was frustrating. How were we supposed to bring in new young people when we treated the young people we did have like they were a nuisance? And these were good kids! Really good kids! It pisses me off to think about some of the things that were said to and about them . . .[1]

Derrick's experience is hardly an isolated one. Millennial church-goers and church visitors—you have not been imagining it. Older churchgoers and church members—we younger generations who have looked up to you also see you. We see the way you cringe when a child of ours makes the slightest bit of noise. We see the sideways scowls at the mother who is breastfeeding her child. We hear the disapproval when someone passive-aggressively mentions, "You know, some people have been saying that the behavior/clothing/language/

---

1. Derrick L. Weston, "What Broke Me," *https://derricklweston.com/2015/01/18/what-broke -me/*, January 18, 2015, last accessed December 15, 2017.

demeanor of these new visitors is not really appropriate at this church, and we thought that you should know that."

All of those little interactions add up. They become the pile of straw on the proverbial camel's back before the final straw breaks it. Individually, such comments may simply fray a nerve or nag at our consciences, but collectively, they are the reason younger people may fall away from a congregation because of what is being communicated about the ossified culture of that particular community. Some go on to join other faith families. Others drop out of the body of Christ altogether.

When a generational monoculture takes hold in a congregation, and only one generation holds sway, what can result is a level of toxic homogeneity that is stifling to millennials. One of my generational-peer colleagues in professional ministry shared on the condition of anonymity this particular recollection of her ministry:

> [I'm in] Sunday school class where the youngest person not paid to be here is seventy years old, talking about "kids today" as the "me" generation who think they are the only thing that matters in the world and [how] all the grandparents in the room "need to set them straight" . . . We actually had a guy say, "I don't want a bunch of young people coming here."
>
> I wonder why there aren't younger folks in the room?

Millennials hear these established churchgoers loud and clear. And, to rephrase Michelle Obama's oft-repeated refrain of "When they go low, we go high": when the church goes low, millennials go out the door.

Lest, by this point in this chapter, I simply sound like I am grousing about what older generations think of the whipper-snappers, let me be clear: this phenomenon is not limited to the elderly, or to the baby boomers, or to any generation. The tendency of church pastors today to pick one subset of a generation (such as, for instance, left-handed soccer moms whose last names begin and end with the same letter and who were born under a new moon— and I am only slightly exaggerating the extent to which these target

demographics are picked) and go all-in on trying to woo that particular demographic can result in the same sort of toxic homogeneity
that shuns the outsider who does not look and talk like them.

Any of the generations within the church can fall prey to such
toxic homogeneity—and that includes millennials. It can wreak
destruction upon the church by quashing its welcome towards the
immigrant, whoever that immigrant may be—a member of a younger
generation, someone of a different race or ethnicity, or a member
of a different socio-economic status. A deep-seated need to maintain the uniform look or feel of a parish's membership is antithetical
to the surrender to true community that being the body of Christ
requires of us as Christians.

When Surrender Involves Sacrifice

We talked together in the last chapter about some of the financial
realities that the millennial generation has faced. Such a conversation about money would be incomplete without also discussing the
financial realities that churches face, and how those realities might
reflect how a church values the future ranks of its membership rolls.

Because of the economic realities many of my own millennial-
aged congregants have faced, I knew that expecting a 10 percent
gross income tithe from them was out of the question. But it did not
stop pastors like me from still hearing the mean-spirited comments
from older parishioners seeking to get their way on this issue or that
board decision. "Who do you think really pays for this church?"
"You think the next generation is going to pay the bills?" And the
all-encompassing, "I have heard that people are complaining about
all of the young people here. . . ."

Every single pastor I have spoken to finds these sorts of conversations terribly demoralizing, for a variety of reasons. None of us
went into ministry hoping to cater to our peoples' selfish impulses.
At worst, these expressions represent a form of blackmail, since tithes
pay our salaries, and saying "Who do you think really pays for this
church?" is an unsubtle way of communicating, "Do not forget who

pays you." The selfishness behind these comments is antithetical to the gospel teaching that we are meant to put our interests and desires second and to lead by serving, not by demanding to be served. Otherwise, Christ's teaching that the first shall be last and the last shall be first needs to be accompanied with a giant asterisk and the disclaimer, "Does not apply to all parts of the body of Christ."

Millennial families see that disclaimer acted out in all sorts of ways in a church's budget for its ministries and programs. I once received a letter in the mail from a neighboring church's senior ministry promoting a guest speaker whose presentation sounded extremely interesting, even potentially life-changing. The letter stated, "all are welcome," but immediately beneath that were the words, "no nursery care provided." Church events and worship services that eschew nursery care for young children are not events where "all are welcome," full stop.

I have colleagues whose church boards have slashed the proposed nursery care budget to the bone, or eliminated it altogether. Budgets are moral, theological documents. As Jesus taught in the heart of the Sermon on the Mount, "Where your treasure is, there your heart will be also" (Matthew 6:21). Show me a budget, and I will show you the priorities of whomever that budget belongs to, be it a person or an organization. We may not always feel comfortable talking about money in church, yet in church, money is still what talks. Words proclaiming welcome on a marquee only whisper, for they represent only a very small sacrifice. Again, I would draw from Jesus's words: "Be careful that you don't practice your religion in front of people to draw their attention. If you do, you will have no reward from your Father who is in heaven" (Matthew 6:1). If we practice our faith in a certain way so as to try to get the attention of a generation, or to try to communicate to them a welcome while in private we practice a very different sort of faith, then according to Jesus, we may well be jeopardizing our own divine rewards.

A critical question the current church must answer is if it is truly ready to surrender its wants and preferences to the church that is to come. To return to the differences between a greenhorn and a trail leader in *Oregon Trail*, an ideal trail leader surrenders their personal wants in order to do what is best to lead the whole wagon train, not just their individual constituency. Until we in the church can so willingly and prophetically surrender ourselves to the joy of community in not just the current church but also the future church, we will continue to remain lost, which is what happens when any group follows an influence that is leading it down an increasingly rougher trail.

The Current and Future Church

Back on the trail, though, we as Christians should be excited about the future church. It consists of not just the ones we gain through birth, but also the people who have not yet made that tentative toe-dip or embrace into the fold, but who might one day. Yet our expression of preferences almost always prioritizes the current church over its future incarnations. My personal favorite might be, "It is not like the future church is paying our bills right now." Perhaps not, but one day, we will be.

It should come as little surprise that millennials see their passions as wholly separate from the passions of the church. Millennials, as you have probably surmised so far from the statistical data and quotations I have presented, are often very interested in taking an existing institution and using it to do something new. If what we are asked to do is simply to prop up said institution, our interest and inspiration rapidly dries up.

If we are going to be asked to "save" the church, then, rather than "kill" it along with Styrofoam cups, Applebee's, Radio Shack, and Sears & Roebuck (ours is a particularly long and impressive path of destruction), our vision for what the church could one day be *must* start to be taken into account. Expecting us to save the existing church and then dictating to us the vision we are expected to adhere to is a losing proposition, because that vision is not built upon the gifts of our generation, which is being asked to run onto the field and deliver something akin to a miracle play. If you want the generation rising after you to succeed, it should be obvious to put them in the best position possible to do so. But that has not always happened within the church, and as a result, we are now reaping what we have spent years—even decades—sowing.

Concern for the current church has so eclipsed every other priority within American Christianity that it has infected even the present stampede to build the church of the future. The church of the future is expected to be built with the tools of the church of the present, and in the image of the church of the past. Yet if that were the approach that Jesus Christ took to his own ministry, I remain firmly convinced that his ministry would have never expanded past first-century Galilee, and almost certainly would not still exist in twenty-first century America.

It is not wrong to ask millennials today to nurture a church for the future. Quite the opposite. But the mandate for that monumental task must be accompanied by the freedom to reshape the church not in its current image or past images, but in the image of a God who is as ready as we are to witness what manner of God-honoring, Jesus-following, people-loving mission the beloved community might become.

The Courage to Resurrect—Together

The resurrection stories in the Gospels are, for me, among the most important ones the Gospels tell—Jairus's daughter in Mark 5, Lazarus in John 11, and, of course, Christ's own resurrection to which all four Gospels attest. Without the resurrection of the Lord, we almost certainly would never have heard of him and his ministry. He would have been another in a long list of troublesome Israelites executed by Caesar's government. And the resurrections of Jairus's daughter and especially of Lazarus set the table for the resurrection of Jesus by demonstrating even earlier in Jesus's public ministry that the promise of God's love is capable of conquering earthly death.

But these three resurrections—of Jesus, Lazarus, and Jairus's daughter—are all solo acts. Each resurrection takes place separately from the other two. On the one hand, that allows for full focus from both the respective evangelist and their audience on the miracle for that individual person. On the other hand, these separate stories occur so far apart from one another in the Gospels that it is easy to see them as separate stories, unconnected by the larger narrative of divinely given new life that intimately intertwines them.

Were we to view the resurrections of an anonymous daughter and the brother of Mary and Martha not only as wholly separate occurrences but also as a commonly shared part of a community of newfound Jesus followers, it becomes possible for us to view resurrection as an inherently communal, rather than solitary, act of receiving the grace and love of God. Even when we speak of resurrection of a community such as a parish or congregation, that resurrection is still often spoken of in an individual sense, of this one community resurrecting itself without much thought or regard for its own symbiotic connections within the wider church.

As long as we continue to worship at, belong to, and preach the church of independence, those inherently limiting frames of reference towards resurrection will endure. We will continue to not see resurrection fully, in all its dimensions, if it remains to us a primarily individual act. Moving from being a church of independence to a church of *inter*dependence, with all the sacrifice of the individual self that such a metamorphosis entails, may give us hope anew to view our relationship with God not merely as a personal relationship but as a universal relationship, enveloping with ease and with truth all facets of our collective existence.

Such surrender to the whole church, and to the inevitabilities of time and generational change, is a difficult task, I know. I do not expect it from anyone, or any congregation, overnight. But it is what I would hope most for from the universal church over time— that we would resurrect *together.*

Chapter 3

Fording the River
Plunging Forth into New Territory

Let there be light.

When the earth was without form, and void, and chaos covered the deep, Genesis says, God spoke those sacred words. Thus, creation began, with light and dark, sea and sky, sun and moon bursting forth from nothing but God's own voice. And God saw that it was good.

Let there be light.

It is Monday, August 21, 2017—Solar Eclipse Day. My wife awakens at 4:00 am to drive down to Salem, Oregon, to be in the path of totality, but, as an at least nominally normal person, I cannot bring myself to arise at so torturously early an hour. Instead, I drive just several miles south to Fort Vancouver with one of my in-laws, Ron, to watch the eclipse at 99 percent totality there, surrounded by the beauty that is a national park nestled in the heart of my adopted hometown.

Ron and I unfurl our beach towels on a patch of green grass and wait for the eclipse to start. I notice, a few paces to my right, two young women who each came to the eclipse by themselves. One of them came prepared with a blanket, hat, drinks, and lawn chair. The other is empty-handed. The first woman offers the other her blanket to share. The other is hesitant, but ultimately accepts. They scoot together. Soon, they're talking away, breaking the ice as only complete strangers brought together by a special event can. It is clear, even from a short distance away, that each of them is increasingly enjoying the other's company.

Let there be light.

The eclipse begins, slowly at first, but then more noticeably as the sun is reduced to a sliver around the moon's silhouette. I remember spotting many of the heroes of Greek mythology in the constellations as a child, and I begin to wonder if today I might see something—metaphorically, at least—of Icarus, the daring and impetuous young man who flew high, far too high, into the sun's path. His is a story of the headstrong vitality of youth that, for me, has always invoked both a dash of inspiration and a touch of dread. His light shone brightly, so much so that it kept him from respecting the great light that shines above him and me alike.

Being several miles away from the path of complete totality grants me the space for not just mythological but also theological reflection. The light shines in the darkness, says John the Evangelist at the start of his Gospel, and the darkness cannot overcome it. Even with 99 percent of its illumination blotted out by the moon, the sun's light is not wholly overcome. And even in the path of totality, that light is only overcome for a scant few magical, mystical minutes.

Let there be light.

With the eclipse now waning, the woman who had lent her blanket gets up to depart. The other prepares to give the blanket back, and the first woman hastens to say, "No, please keep it. Today was a gift. This, too, is a gift." They exchange names and embrace. For a moment, the growing brightness of the sun is shadowed not by the moon, but by this genuine display of affection. The first woman goes about her way. The other sits back down, and curls up on the blanket that is now hers, utterly content for now to bask in the light of both God's good creation and the love of human hearts. And I have to think that God saw that it was good.

Let there be light.

Faced with an as-yet historically unique set of circumstances—a world made smaller than ever with the quantum leaps forward in digital technology and social media, yet also made poorer by the ripple-effect repercussions of the global financial collapse of a decade ago—millennials have adapted by becoming nomadic for different reasons than our predecessors. Our habits of where to live—and of when to pull up stakes to move there—can lead to fleeting connections with other people. This trend is not necessarily by design; rather, it exists simply as a byproduct of the lifestyle we lead, in no small part out of economic necessity as chapter one illustrated.

One consequence this fundamental change in lifestyle entails is, like the young woman giving up her blanket at the solar eclipse, an emphasis on experiencing life rather than accumulating it. By that I mean because so many carrots dangled before millennials (such as home ownership and steady employment) have not readily materialized as they did for previous generations, their value has decreased to many of us, and likewise our commitment to them has waned rapidly.

This is not to say that they have no value—my wife and I just bought our first home a couple of years ago—only that they are valued differently. The prototypical American dream of a house, picket fence, a carful of children, and every other trapping from the Game of LIFE® is no longer the be-all-end-all for our generation. It stands to reason, then, that the prototypical American dream for a neighborhood church—a vast, yet also impeccably maintained building with every classroom full to bursting with children done up in their Sunday best as their parents attend teas, bunco, and raffles led by the pastor's wife (not husband)—will likewise have changed over the years.

The historical Oregon Trail represented a similar metamorphosis of the American dream for nineteenth-century pioneers, such as it existed back then. Rather than try to build on what little they may have had in their previous hometowns, they moved to Independence, Missouri, and then set out across a wilderness that did not belong to them in search of something different.

But to do so, they first had to cross the Missouri and Kansas Rivers, the first in a lineup of fierce currents that bisected the Oregon Trail at various points. Those rivers became notorious for the dangers they posed to the pioneers. Yet traverse those rivers they did, by the wagonload.

The Dangers of Fording the River

Firmly ensconced within the wagon train, and with Independence in the rearview mirror, the dangers, privations, and eventualities of the Oregon Trail came into focus for both the nineteenth-century pioneers and their twentieth- and twenty-first-century progeny playing the eponymous video game. Rivers that required fording, food that required rationing, and wild game that required hunting all posed challenges, yet while decisions concerning rations and wagon pace could be made by the player, the results of crossing a river were partially player-determined and partially luck-driven.

Faced with a shallow river, an erstwhile pioneer sitting at their computer screen could ford the stream with their team of oxen and hope for the best. For deeper and more treacherous currents, the option of caulking the wagon and floating it across the river was the preferable choice. Occasionally, a player could essentially enter a cheat code to increase their chances of safe passage by splurging several dollars or a few sets of clothes for a ferry or a guide from the Shoshone tribe to usher them across the river. In retrospect, the use of American Indians as non-player character "guides" solely to enable the player's progress was particularly problematic; we will talk about the Manifest Destiny/Doctrine of Discovery attitude behind such approaches towards American Indians in chapter seven.

Both fording and caulking led to a tense several seconds of held breaths, crossed fingers, and prayers to the video game gods. We all hoped to not see our wagons tip over into the pixelated blue current of whatever river stood between us and the Willamette Valley. On an elementary level, I imagine getting to this part of the game with a group of your friends was the type of collective effervescence that religious anthropologist Émile Durkheim wrote of in his landmark 1912 work *The Elementary Forms of Religious Life*: as a group, we were so caught up in the energy and suspense of this ritual within the shared experience of the game that the collective nature of it amplified both the energy and the feelings of suspense.[1] Understood through such a lens, any number of things—including playing a basic-yet-addictive video game—could potentially be interpreted as spiritual experiences, even outside the confines of a parish.

It is the confines of the parish, however, to which congregations continue to ask new seekers to commit themselves. Even with the "You are now entering the mission field" sort of lip service congregations preach about the importance of being church in the wider community and not just within the four walls of the sanctuary, congregations often approach newcomers with the mentality of a mid-twentieth-century corporation: that a person signs on to work for them as a young adult and continues with that outfit all the way to riding off into the sunset of retirement—with a full pension, of course.

There are many other ways in which congregations have come to resemble corporations. Think of how often you hear comparisons of a pastor to a CEO, or of how the church should be run more like a business. We will be exploring some of those aspects in chapter six, which concerns how millennial styles of leadership can vary dramatically from the corporate models of leadership embraced by the baby boomers. For now, it suffices to say that there are ways in which congregations can learn from a corporate mindset, but the approach of treating potential members like new job hires is emphatically not one of them—especially when the entire notion of church membership is increasingly fraught with spiritual and intergenerational tension.

Corporations and churches are both often seen as paragons of stability, even though neither ought to be. After all, we are only one short decade past the events that triggered the greatest economic crisis since the Great Depression, and while churches should embrace their past, it remains true that throughout the church's storied history, congregations are at their best when they are in states of movement and even metamorphosis rather than stasis.

---

1. Émile Durkheim, *The Elementary Forms of Religious Life*, ed. Mark S. Cladis, trans. Carol Cosman (Oxford University Press, 2008), 296.

The Pentecost story the church remembers and celebrates every spring, fifty days after Easter, is a story of such movement. The Holy Spirit did not fall upon the faithful in their own separate longstanding congregations. Rather, the dove descended upon fellow travelers, wayfarers, and pilgrims who had journeyed far to arrive at Jerusalem. The Holy Spirit came first not to the landed church and its socially prominent pastor with a solid, firm pulpit surrounded by a grand edifice of a sanctuary, but to a collection of journeyers of so little importance to their contemporaries that we know none of their names, save for the twelve apostles.

We should not be surprised that a manifestation of the same God who sent Christ—the Christ who told his disciples to set aside everything and follow him, who told the young rich man to sell everything and come with him, that he would have treasure in heaven—would come to spiritual nomads. If the Son of Man has no place to lay his head, as Jesus says in both Matthew 8 and Luke 9, then why would the Holy Spirit not grace the anonymous, uprooted masses instead of the landed gentry?

Such is the nomadic nature of the Holy Spirit, unbounded by the physical restrictions of humanity. And under that same Spirit's providence, we millennial believers are often quite purposeful in living out our status as nomads as we fashion for ourselves a way of being spiritual that does not depend on remaining for years in the exact same worship spaces.

Purposeful Nomads

Surprisingly, millennials relocate less frequently than our predecessors. Only one in five of those ages twenty-five to thirty-five reported living at a different address from the previous year.[2] Yet we are still less apt to put down roots when we move compared to

---

2. Richard Fry, "Americans Are Moving at Historically Low Rates, in Part Because Millennials Are Staying Put," *Pew Research Center*, *http://www.pewresearch.org/fact-tank/2017/02/13 /americans-are-moving-at-historically-low-rates-in-part-because-millennials-are-staying-put/*, February 13, 2017, last accessed December 15, 2017.

past generations, as two in five millennials have moved somewhere for reasons other than college with the intention of not permanently settling there.[3] Additionally, while roughly three in ten of all millennials say that they have relocated for an age-old reason—a job—almost as many report relocating for lifestyle reasons or a new experience.[4]

Lost in the shuffle are traditional reasons for relocating, like a spouse's job or home ownership, because we have been forced to delay those milestones of young adulthood as a part of our adaptation to the economy we grew into. According to the research cited on this page, those rationales for picking up and moving are far down on the list of reasons why millennials relocate. Even so, we are still tagged as nomads, which ought not to be such a bad thing, but throughout much of history has often been treated as such. Nomads are frequently viewed as stateless and incapable of, or unwilling to, pledge allegiance to a landed nation or community. That view has led to substantial prejudice towards such peoples, from shepherds in the time of Jesus to peoples such as the Romani today.

Shepherds in ancient Israel were wandering wayfarers who moved from place to place for their flocks to graze, sometimes deleteriously so. If you have ever watched a flock of sheep munch on a field of grass, you know what I mean. Shepherds fulfilled an important job in ancient Israel, but that does not mean they were admired.

Yet Jesus refers to himself in John 10 as the Good Shepherd—one of the purposeful *ego eimi* ("I am") statements sprinkled throughout John's Gospel. Given Jesus's use in Luke's Gospel of the Good Samaritan as a vehicle for questioning Judean prejudices against Samaritans, it is hardly a stretch to think that this, too, represents him pointedly questioning a landed society's prejudices towards its nomads and attempting to reframe the label assigned to them. Jesus has a tendency

---

3. "Millennials Favor 'Vacation Moves,'" Mayflower Transit, *https://www.mayflower.com /contact-mayflower/news/vacation-moves-insights*, April 11, 2017, last accessed December 16, 2017.

4. Ibid.

to use the *ego eimi* pronouncements in John to push the envelope with his original audiences, but we now largely take them for granted, with no unfavorable associations attached to them.

If Jesus could see the innate value in living nomadically, the church must be willing to countenance a serious conversation about whether it has strayed from the mission of the itinerant carpenter-turned-Savior whom we call the Messiah. Our mythology consists not so much of, say, the "primeval history" of Genesis—the name attached to its first eleven chapters which document the creation, flood, and Babel narratives—but of the white picket fence, well-manicured lawn, tastefully appointed single-unit house, and requisite number of children. And, crucially, this ideal has served as the church's own mythology for decades: an image—a mirage—of financial stability and material longevity in a world that increasingly projects anything but.

For millennials, the lifestyle trappings like that white picket fence, well-manicured lawn, and children are being replaced with years of renting, at-will or freelance employment, and the postponement of child-rearing. Instead of constructing homes that prominently display our worldly possessions, millennials have adapted to the instability of nomadic life by accumulating a repository of experiences that lives on, yes, in our Instagram accounts and our Facebook albums, but also, more crucially, in our memories.

Combine this tendency of millennials to prefer accumulating experiences to accumulating material possessions with our limited employment prospects—especially those that could afford us the same level of financial security of our parents and grandparents—and you have a generation that is eminently prepared to shoulder the task of reframing the functions of community. Rather than demanding permanence in everything from a style of worship to the worship space itself, the church can take from its millennial cohort a willingness to experiment, an openness to being uprooted, and a commitment to, well, a lack of commitment.

None of that is as scary as it sounds.

Uncommitted to Commitment

One of my maxims when discussing stewardship within the context of congregational ministry has long been, "Show me your calendar and your credit card statement, and I will tell you what you value." I cannot claim credit for being the first to postulate this, but I can testify to how strongly it applies to not only individuals, but groups as well—including churches.

If you belong to a congregation, look at how it spends its time, money, and other resources on outreach, hospitality, and the other ministries that typically overlap with strategies for church growth. Are they line items in the church budget? If so, how well are they funded relative to other programs, groups, and ministries? If not, why are they not funded? What sorts of these ministries has your congregation deemed worth funding, and which have they not? An outreach ministry that provides spiritual care to the residents of a nursing home is incredibly worthwhile—it is something my congregation's praise band in Longview did every year—but what about fostering an outreach ministry whose presence was in the coffeehouses, bars, and performance spaces that younger people outside of the church tend to frequent? Would the former have a better chance than the latter of being approved, much less written into the following year's budget?

Here is another thought experiment. Which tends to be the tougher way to save money if you are a part of a congregation's leadership team that has been tasked with staying on budget for the year: critically reevaluating an existing program with a storied past but that may have run its course, or vetoing a proposed new program that may not be as committed to the template of the rest of the church's programming slate, even though it holds promise for meeting an emerging spiritual need in the community?

None of this should be construed as a fusillade against the virtues of continuity—only against the elevation of continuity to a sacred calf that, like the golden calf of old, draws us away from the mission to which God calls us in favor of our own human preferences. In committing ourselves to a certain way of doing church, we have somehow ended up trapping ourselves in that commitment. We have doubled down on the golden calf of our brand of church, worshiping it rather than worshiping God. All the while, new and exciting ways of being church lie just across the riverbank and further down the trail.

Is it possible, then, for a church to move away from its sacred cow of "commitment"—like the brand loyalty to a denomination or an implied cultural expectation to sign on to a particular congregation right away—and towards, paradoxically, a commitment to being uncommitted to commitment? I would submit that such a move is not only possible, albeit difficult, but an imperative if the church is to adapt to the frontier where millennial Christians already are living. The church must be willing to ford the river to join them on the banks of the water's other side.

The River Itself: The Frontier Millennial Christians Face—And How We're Ready

The crux of the challenge that both spiritually inclined millennials and the wider church face is to leave the confines of the familiar and adapt to the ways of one another, even as those ways continue to change and evolve. Like groups of families forming into wagon trains, such an enterprise looks like a monumental undertaking, especially for a young person who has felt ostracized or alienated from the church of their childhood, or for a church so wedded to its traditions that it has become an unwitting artifact of its former community. I cannot, will not, and do not minimize that challenge; this book is premised on the belief that our frontier is soul-sized in its dimensions. Nothing less than mutual love, inspired by the Holy Spirit, is at stake.

For the millennial who was shunned by their church over their sexuality, political views, or doubts, the frontier is one of reconciliation— one that may not yet be possible because of the harm inflicted or the largely unrepentant stance of much of the Christianity that is most visible in the media today. For the church in turn, the frontier is one of repentance. Yet time and again, I find that it is my generation, not my church (not to be confused with the congregations I have served), that is more equipped to strike out into this frontier because of our appetite for honesty. The disillusionment of my generation comes as much from the church's repeated denials of its destructive behavior and beliefs as from the behavior and beliefs themselves.

This phenomenon becomes a pattern, which in turn becomes a cycle. Young people have justifiably accused the church of any number of institutional sins: racism, sexism, homophobia, transphobia, xenophobia—the list is a shamefully long one. Some millennials, myself included, seek to remedy this litany of wrongs by making change from within. Others head straight for the exits, vowing never to return. Still others watch warily from a distance, believing just enough in the church to not give up on it entirely, but not quite enough to risk making themselves vulnerable by opening up to a congregation. Each group deserves mention.

To my fellow young(ish) idealists who have remained to create the church we believe in out of one which has not always believed in us, thank you, thank you, thank you. I know you have gone through many of the same existential crises that I have over whether it is worth your youth to endeavor to be this breath of fresh air that the church needs you to be. Rest assured, it is.

To my generational peers who have given up on the church completely, I am so sorry. We—the church—have failed you. Full. Stop. I hope you are able to forgive us someday, on your timetable and on your terms, and I hope that the church becomes more willing to do the hard work necessary to reconcile with you.

And to the millennials who are taking a wait-and-see approach to the church, I hope you are able one day to feel confident and secure enough to ford the river, to take the leap of faith, and that far from your own wagon tipping over and spilling your life's contents, you arrive safely on the other side of the waters, surrounded by the great cloud of witnesses who cheered you across.

Each of us has responded, reacted, and adapted to the institutional church in different and valid ways. Far from exhibiting the immaturity our generation is often tagged with, each response shows a deep sense of understanding of who we are and of our relationship with the body of Christ—not what it used to be or what our elders would like for it to be. Even if your response does not fit nicely and neatly into one of the three outlined here, or if it combines components from more than one, we continue to live out one of the most critical lessons we were taught as children: don't give in to social expectations or peer pressure.

That common denominator in each of our responses to the institutional church ought to underscore the preparedness of millennials to one day lead the church across the river ourselves. I cannot promise that we will be as talented as we would like to be at what is being expected of us. The shouldering of the church's weight is a herculean task for any generation, but doubly so when that generation has not been offered either the opportunities or the resources to do so effectively and faithfully. But what I do feel confident in promising is that millennials will continue our relationship, or lack thereof, with Christianity from a place of fundamental honesty and authenticity, which means we will not always talk or behave in ways that our predecessors did, or want us to. Then again, younger generations have always confounded the expectations of older generations.

But millennials cannot be asked by our predecessors to save something that those predecessors still claim ownership over if we are not allowed to negotiate our own terms for doing so. That is not a compromise—that is a one-sided sacrifice of one generation's spiritual needs on behalf of another's, like Abraham's attempt to sacrifice his son Isaac upon the altar.

The frontier millennials face is one of sacrificing in order to redefine the church and its relationship with us. Far too often, however, we are asked to unilaterally sacrifice our religious wants. We are being asked to preserve something—the church—as it once was, like a time capsule from decades past that may no longer reflect its community, without the opportunity to impart our own imprint on it.

Those are not terms any generation should have to accept to revitalize anything. Is it any wonder, then, that millennials have responded by collectively turning down that offer? It is not so much that millennials are not ready to cross into the great unknown of the frontier, but that the church may not quite yet be ready to cross into that frontier with us.

That reluctance on the part of Christianity requires a remedy—one that I am by no means the first to suggest.

Another Great Awakening

Rob Lee IV, the millennial pastor who made headlines in 2017 with his explicit disavowal of his ancestor Robert E. Lee's Confederate legacy, writes in his own treatment of millennial spirituality, *Stained Glass Millennials*, that he sees our generation as potentially standing before a historical era of Reformation-esque dimensions, saying, "[R]arely does so much rest on the future of the institutional church as it seems to here and now. The millennial generation is called in a time that presents the opportunity to join the ranks of the great reformers of the church, from Luther to Calvin to Wesley."[5]

I am not sure that I would go so far as to declare this an era of another Reformation, although it is tempting to do so in the wake of the five-hundredth anniversary of Martin Luther's Reformation that was commemorated in 2017. Perhaps it is the impostor syndrome in me, but I would hardly put myself—or any of us millennial Christians—in the same category as Luther, Calvin, or Zwingli quite yet.

But I am confident that something tremendous is indeed needed from my generation, as well as from Generation X, that may well end up being another Great Awakening of sorts. American Christendom has already experienced at least three Great

---

5. Rob Lee, *Stained Glass Millennials* (Macon, GA: Smyth & Helwys Publishing Incorporated, 2017), 21.

Awakenings, during the mid-1700s, early 1800s, and late 1800s, respectively. Some religious scholars consider the reshuffling of the church that took place from the 1960s to the early 1980s, with the rapid resurgence of evangelical Christianity, followed by its dramatically increased partisanship on the side of the Republican Party, as a fourth Great Awakening.

Yet the Great Awakening needed now is not one that is as wrathful and punishing as the first preached by fire-breathing pastors like Jonathan Edwards, or as fueled by Manifest Destiny and the Doctrine of Discovery as the second, or as puritanical and unforgiving as the temperance movements that propelled the third. What is needed now is a Great Awakening built not on the expectations of Americana as the previous three or four have been, but on the exhortations of Jesus and those closest to him. In short, we need a Great Awakening from a generation that loves Jesus but not necessarily the church.

James, the brother of Jesus, used his letter in the New Testament to call on the early church to stand up for the poor and the oppressed, to strive to change the behavior of their oppressors, and to be the tongues that blessed in an era of curses and a coarse disregard for love. Paul, in his letters to Philemon and the church in Corinth, implored Christians to welcome the oppressed not as slaves to human masters, but as siblings in Christ bought with a divine, not human, price. And Jesus taught in Matthew 22:40 that the entirety of the Law and the Prophets hangs upon love of God and love of neighbor. Can the revival of the realm of God come based on these principles, rather than on the principles of Great Awakenings past?

If such a revival is to come about, I believe it will not only be because millennials decide not to abandon the church, but also because more of us will begin to see that the church is again incarnating Jesus's call for generosity and compassion, rather than adhering to our petty partisan preferences.

Think back to the story of the two women enjoying one another's company during the solar eclipse. A simple act of generosity turned a pair of strangers into friends. Nothing about such generosity need be Christian in order to make a positive impact upon another's life, but what if it were? What if being known for such generosity of spirit was once more among the most prominent of Christian values?

For a generation that values experience so highly to have not experienced generosity and compassion from the church is a terrible witness. The church may be doomed to irrelevancy as a result unless it reorients its moral compass and opens itself to the winds of revitalization that a Great Awakening led by the millennials and Gen X-ers could portend.

Such a movement might not be a panacea for American Christianity, but it would call the church to ford a river that flows with the living water that Jesus teaches of in the Gospels.

Starting—and Ending—with Genesis

Let there be light.
And there was light. And God saw that the light was good.

Creation after creation, from the oceans and the lands to the sun and the moon and the stars and humanity itself, God crafted it all out of nothing but words, and then proclaimed it to be good.

We end this chapter by returning to the creation story in Genesis 1, the story I could not help reflecting on the day of the solar eclipse as I gave thanks for humanity and creation alike. Yet Genesis 1 is a chapter that, like so many other Bible stories, has been saddled with partisan baggage as a vehicle for doctrinaire Christians to revive the grievances of the Scopes Monkey Trial and the harsh fundamentalism of young earth creationism.

I barely saw Charles Darwin's theory of evolution taught as a public high school student in Kansas because, at that time, the state school board was controlled by such strict and unyielding Christians that they wanted no such scientific blasphemy uttered in a biology classroom. Evolution was removed from the state curriculum a year before I began high school.[6] The first time I read anything by Darwin, I was a junior in college, and it was in modern European history, not biology—all because a small group of fundamentalist Christians in positions of earthly power decided to turn a beautiful creation story into a political line in the sand.

It is one of many self-inflicted body blows the church's reputation has taken in the past several decades, and one that is indicative of Christians' often collective tendency to sacrifice the well-being of others on the altar of doctrinal purity. That tendency has, time and again, added to the baggage that must now be unpacked, sorted, and, frankly, apologized for if the church is to have a future in my generation, for with that baggage has come a great deal of chaos. After decades of worshiping both stability and doctrinal purity, congregations across the country have struggled to survive and even closed their doors because of a sudden uncertainty about their futures.

That reality ought to impress upon the church that we are already in the middle of the river. The waters that God splits in Genesis 1 were seen by a great many primeval peoples, not just the ancient Israelites, as a source of chaos, uncertainty, and destruction—just as the great rivers that bisected the Oregon Trail were seen as sources of uncertainty and potential destruction for the pioneers.

There is something awe-inspiring about God cleaving apart that great source of chaos—not just in Genesis 1, but in the Exodus narrative at the Red Sea so that God's children might be liberated from the bonds of slavery. Those stories should inspire awe in us, and a reverence for God's creative abilities, rather than a strict adherence to relatively recent doctrines cooked up for political purposes. The former is glorious to behold; the latter is simply more baggage. Like the church, stories such as the creation saga need to be shed of that baggage and reclaimed to be what God had always intended: lenses through which God could be glimpsed, approached, and worshiped.

---

6. Pam Belluck, "Board for Kansas Deletes Evolution from Curriculum," *New York Times*, *http://www.nytimes.com/1999/08/12/us/board-for-kansas-deletes-evolution-from-curriculum.html*, August 12, 1999, last accessed February 21, 2018.

Yet no lens, however great its scope, can be as helpful as it ought to be in seeing what needs to be seen if it has been distorted beyond its creator's original specifications. Paul Tillich, the twentieth-century German-American theologian, taught that all the items that point us towards God in our life—the scriptures, the church, our own experience, even Jesus himself—are lenses or windows through which to see God.[7] And while God inspired our divine lenses, we are the ones charged with their well-being. As Adam and Eve were charged with stewardship of the earth, so too are we charged with stewardship of how God is revealed to us.

In our care for those lenses, we are presented with choices that define who we are. Sometimes, those choices are life-changing in their significance, forever altering the direction of our life's journey. Other times, they seem minor on the surface, but carry far more weight than initially meets the eye: a simple act of kindness, the spark of a potential friendship, shaped in the shadow of a once-in-a-generation eclipse. The choosing of relationship over possession of a resource does not have to create impoverishment. Quite the contrary, it can lead us toward new riches.

The church can elect to recycle the same means and methods that have produced the results that have much of American Christianity wailing in lament at its dwindling relevancy. Nothing is stopping us from doing so. If the church wishes to continue emphasizing the narrow wealth of material resources and longevity over interconnection and experience, we are free to do so.

Or Christianity can choose to cross over to new means and methods. Jesus followers can choose to ford the river that God calls us to both cross and care for, along with all the other lands, waters, and air that make up this wondrous, beautiful, fragile, enduring planet that is our frontier. Christians can choose to cross over to new ways of building community, many of which millennials already embrace.

---

7. Kate Braestrup, *Marriage and Other Acts of Charity: A Memoir* (Reagan Arthur/Back Bay Books, 2011), 102.

The following chapters detail a number of ways in which millennials—and especially millennials of faith—have embraced new methods of creating ad hoc spiritual communities, whether online, in moments of crisis, or through a shared common cause. To share them with you is not simply a means of learning what it is kids these days are up to, but of celebrating and affirming what we are creating and caring about, and what we have found to be most important. Life. Love. Passion. Fulfillment. And a faith that we may choose to express differently, but one that is as strong and vital as that of any generation before ours.

God authored such things as far back as the creation stories of Genesis. In these stories, we are told, God created such things for us. Not for us to exploit, but for us to see, just as God saw when they were first made that they were good. Not mediocre. Not adequate. Not fair-to-middling. Good.

These were the words and deeds of God before any of us in our fragile human vessels came to be, in all our splendor and brokenness.

May they continue to be the words of God before our own deeds that light the way forward for one another as we walk along the trail—and ford the river—together.

Let there be light.

Chapter 4

Hunting for Food
Two Hundred Pounds of Spiritual Nourishment

Santa is an obese elderly man who gets chauffeured not just from con-
tinent to continent but house to house and lives on a diet of cookies.
The Easter Bunny would have agility, stamina, and possibly rabies on
its side. Santa would be toast.[1]

I have been on the website Reddit for over four years, attempting
to constructively contribute to several different subreddits,[2] and of
all the comments I have made there over the years, the one with the
most upvotes by far was the above answer to the question of who
would win in a fistfight between Santa Claus and the Easter Bunny.

Go figure.

I know, I know—worst generation ever and all that. Believe me,
I have heard it. Constantly.

But Christmas is meant to be a season of joy. If bantering with
strangers from around the world in a thread on the "Ask Me Anything" (AMA) subreddit of Reddit on Christmas Eve was a means

---

1. Eric Atcheson, "It's Christmas Eve, and I'm a parish pastor. AMA!" *https://www.reddit*
.com/r/IAmA/comments/5k36mj/its_christmas_eve_and_im_a_parish_pastor_ama/, December 24,
2016, last accessed December 23, 2017.

2. On Reddit, a "subreddit" is a forum dedicated specifically to a particular subject. For
instance, you might find subreddits for your favorite sports team or your favorite academic
subject, to which people post articles, questions, photos, and other items for discussion.

of providing a little bit of that joy, then it was a far better use of my time than hearing "Baby, It's Cold Outside," "Santa Baby," or, God forbid, "Christmas Shoes" on the radio one more blasted time.

And for a number of the people who used that AMA thread to contact me—both publicly and privately—it was a better use of their time than trying to muster up the emotional and spiritual fortitude to trek back to a church that had already burned them. In so many ways—over their sexuality, their methods of grieving, or any number of other reasons—they were clearly told that they did not fit into the inhumanely tight molds their churches had demanded they fit into throughout their lives.

I made human connections through that AMA. I made new friends whom I would otherwise have never encountered, but with whom I get to converse, and begin to trust, all through social media. I was humbled by the extent to which complete strangers whose faces I had never seen—and likely would never see—were willing to confide in me the difficult emotional and spiritual places in which they found themselves in that Christmas season.

Having exchanged the surroundings of the parish for the climes of spiritual wilderness and frontier, we millennials have added the role of hunter to our repertoires—not so much that spiritual fulfillment is our prey, but that we continue searching for the role it has to play in our lives. To fulfill that role, instead of returning to the settled public squares of our congregations, we are setting out for what is, on the surface, the wilderness of less established and less civilized spiritual territory—the internet and its array of online progeny.

The world of podcasts, recorded sermons, and digitally available worship music makes up a huge swath of this newer spiritual territory, and young seekers are increasingly making that territory a part of their religious home. But this chapter is not about those avenues, most of which are rather straightforward; you can go online, download the content, and watch, read, or listen on your own time. That is often a solo endeavor. It does not need to be, but it often is.

This chapter is about the formation of more multidimensional spiritual arenas online: honest-to-goodness communities that may not resemble traditional churches in their organization and governance—no board of directors with a president, vice president, treasurer, and secretary, and no committees formed to oversee still more communities—but which are managing to make a difference in the lives of millennials where our traditional parishes often struggle. And that difference is often because of, not necessarily in spite of, the ad hoc nature of these digital communities.

Millennials hunt for spiritual food in these digitized frontiers. Sometimes, we come up empty. Other times, we find just enough sustenance to get by. And occasionally, we walk away with enough nourishment to sustain us for days or weeks on end. In this way, at least, our hunting for spiritual food is not so different from traditional church life. But, because it is done mostly on our terms, it is ultimately a different phenomenon and experience.

And if for no other reason than that singular difference, it is important for churches to recognize that accepting millennials is not just tolerating our presence in the pews on Sundays, but tolerating that our presence in the body of Christ is very much not limited to Sunday mornings. Our hunt for food takes place at all manner of points along the trail, not only where generations before us have hunted and found more than enough food to eat. *Oregon Trail* permits a player to bring only two hundred pounds of food back from a hunt, no matter how much game the player shot. A player cannot bring back more in a day and has to keep hunting the next day. But as the game tells you after a day of hunting, if you continue to hunt in the same area, food will become scarce. That is exactly the phenomenon that the millennial generation often experiences when hunting for its spiritual succor. Nourishment has become scarce for us in the institutional church, so we have continued upon the trail.

Creating an Online Character

Let's start with something wildly self-evident: millennials are a plugged-in bunch. In 2015, 90 percent of adults ages 18–29 reported being active on at least one social media website. That number dropped to 86 percent in 2016, but the number of adults ages 30–49—the demographic that millennials are now beginning to age into—who reported being active on at least one social media website rose from 77 percent to 80 percent. These numbers are noticeably higher than those for boomers (ages 50–64) or the silent generation (ages 65+), whose percentages were 51 percent and 35 percent, respectively—although the ages 50–64 demographic experienced a large bump from 2015 to 2016, raising their participation rate to 64 percent,[3] suggesting that Generation X may well share their younger generational siblings' affinity for social media.

The statistics also point to how the excessive use of social media can, ironically, lead to detachment and disconnect in relationship—42 percent of adults ages 18–29 in 2014 said that their partner has been distracted by their mobile device during time spent together, compared to 25 percent of all couples regardless of age. Yet surprisingly, the internet can also help mend those frayed relationships, as 41 percent of young adults say that they are able to feel closer to their partner because of online and digital communication, and 23 percent have used online or digital communication to help resolve a dispute they could not resolve in person.[4] Furthermore, the internet and social media have provided millennials with tools to find new friendships and connections where previously none had existed. In fact, 39 percent of all adults—or 2 in 5—report being friends on social media with someone they have never met in person.[5] I am among those two in five adults—more on my personal experience in a bit.

The millennial generation's status as the most digitized and internet-saturated generation of all time has led to us also generally being the adult generation most used to living out our lives on social

---

3. "Social Media Fact Sheet," *Pew Research Center, http://www.pewinternet.org/fact-sheet /social-media/,* January 12, 2017, last accessed December 18, 2017.

4. Amanda Lenhart and Maeve Duggan, "Couples, the Internet, and Social Media," *Pew Research Center, http://www.pewinternet.org/2014/02/11/couples-the-internet-and-social-media/,* February 11, 2014, last accessed December 18, 2017.

5. Maeve Duggan, Nicole B. Ellison, Cliff Lampe, Amanda Lenhart, and Mary Madden, "Social Media Update: 2014," *Pew Research Center, http://www.pewinternet.org/files/2015/ 01 /PI_SocialMediaUpdate2014_pdf.pdf,* January 9, 2015, last accessed December 18, 2017.

media, from friendships to relationships to work responsibilities and all manner of aspects in between—aspects which continue to rapidly blur from one to the other.

And we are comfortable in doing so. This comfort manifests itself in a wide variety of ways. E-commerce apps like Venmo and Stripe are increasingly common for us to use, even as many parishes remain firmly in the era of offering plates and checkbooks. Online video games allow us to play and compete alongside people literally halfway around the world. And while we may carry memories of pain or distrust from the spiritual communities of our youth, online we can form a new wagon party of acquaintances to experience life with.

That individual congregations can create fishbowl-like bubbles of existence (whether by being a small congregation or a larger congregation with a small group structure) is hardly news. But our ways of coping with those bubbles—such as reaching out beyond them to create completely new online communities—are relatively new, and they are rapidly evolving as millennials grow older and pass the baton of most technologically accustomed generation on to Generation Z.

Millennials are not only often comfortable with living our lives out online, but when we struggle in our relationships with our families or churches of origin, we sometimes see our online circles as safer spaces in which to live our lives. I have no statistical proof, but I can attest from personal experience that for many younger Christians and ex-Christians, online communities are often more trusted than families, relatives, and churches that may have shunned them over their sexuality, politics, or any number of other characteristics that were deemed unacceptable. When we consider the tools that the online world offers to someone who is searching for community, that should hardly be a surprise.

Social media allows us to choose our screen names and, in essence, fashion for ourselves a persona from the ground up. While that freedom and anonymity can be misused to abuse and troll others, it is also a tool that younger generations have embraced to reach out for help. When we feel isolated, ignored, or worse, exiled by our brick-and-mortar communities, being able to reach out through a computer screen to a kindred spirit can offer us a tangible and valuable sense of hope.

Finding Connection Outside of Friends and Family

"How can I reconcile the extremely contradictory nature of modern Christianity? I see normal people as well as politicians and business executives wielding their religion as a weapon against people who are different from [them], rather than actually living the teachings of Christianity like love, compassion, generosity."

"I don't believe in religion, yet I respect all of them and the people that practice them, but for some reason I'm seen as the bad fruit in the family. When I say I respect Muslims or Jews for their views, my Christian family likes to take shots at me because "other religions are wrong," yet I do not see it that way."

"My dad was an alcoholic . . . now he's an overbearing Christian. Life was better when he [was] wasted [rather] than now when I have to hear religious insecurity and complete hatred (homophobia, political insecurity, racism) peddled by religious businessmen."[6]

Many of the questions and stories in my Reddit AMAs have been quite fun for me to answer—like the Easter Bunny-versus-Santa Claus question. The three above were not among them. Each of them made my stomach churn.

Had these stories come from my own congregants, I would have found them immensely painful to hear. Hearing them from strangers, I must report, did not lessen the blow. Millennials have come to care for, empathize with, and minister to one another in online settings. While profound ministry is still done face-to-face, it also takes place across digital distances, underscoring the lengths to which people will go in the hunt for spiritual nourishment. As Christmas

---

6. Atcheson, "It's Christmas Eve, and I'm a parish pastor. AMA!"

Eve ticked into Christmas Day, I tried my sacred best to keep going as the stories of heartbreak at the hands of zealously fundamentalist or hurtful friends and relatives piled up before me. And as the birth of the Incarnation of God's love drew closer, those stories only reinforced my need for Jesus.

The frontier of doing ministry online surprisingly lends itself to profound acts of honesty and vulnerability between complete strangers. You can remain anonymous behind your screen name. You may never physically meet the person on the other side of the screen who is asking for, or offering, help and advice. It is therefore unlikely that the people in your life—people you may well be worried by or afraid of—will learn of what you have said about how they have treated you. All of that combines for a potent mixture of truth-telling and emotion that is not unlike group therapy or a twelve-step session.

The fruit of those Reddit AMA threads continues to be borne in my own life. People who found me on Twitter as a result have become people whose opinions I trust, whom I follow closely in order to hear stories I might not get elsewhere, and with whom I get to interact and converse about all manner of things. They have made my life and spirituality richer.

As difficult as it can be to perform ministry on social media, the rewards are great, much like the risks and rewards of performing ministry in traditional face-to-face contexts. What has changed is the reach for those risks and rewards, which is no longer limited to the confines of a person's local community or context. Nor, frankly, is that reach limited to pastors. Laypersons minister to pastors like me all the time online, just as I minister to them. That, too, is a part of this search for connection that has led millennials outside of the walls of the parishes in which they were brought up, and the city limits of the towns in which they were raised, and into a world we were told could be a dangerous wilderness, full of people looking to do us harm or to take advantage of us. Yet, in the midst of that wilderness, we have also found, and keep finding, ways to emotionally and spiritually sustain ourselves.

We Say, Erm, "Fudge"

I mostly look upon who I was in seminary—an immature and inse-
cure doofus with a massive chip on his shoulder—with utter bewil-
derment at how a pastor managed to emerge, but it was during those
years that I encountered two of the most gifted and patient people I
have ever met.

One is my wife, Carrie. The other is my seminary classmate-
turned-roommate, Jason, whose even keel and enviably laid-back
equilibrium projected an image of maturity and thoughtfulness juxtaposed with my shenanigans—when he wasn't busy enabling them.
Now he ministers to the actively dying and their families as a home
hospice chaplain while his wife, Kelly, pastors a United Church of
Christ congregation in the beautiful Columbia River gorge, a drive
of only an hour or two from Carrie and me in Vancouver. In seminary, his reserves of patience and equanimity were tested alongside
my much less impressive capacity for such composure in the face of
the vagaries of our theological education. One evening, out of nothing more than a state of mutual frustration at our shared circumstance as jaded third-year seminarians, Jason and I created a private,
invitation-only group on Facebook for our classmates and friends
that had, as a part of its name, the word "fudge" (except the actual
word wasn't "fudge," if you get my drift).

Starting with a few of our closest confidants, the group became
an acceptable place for us to unload on whatever frustrated us at the
moment: our field education site, our capstone paper, or even just
the news helicopters that rotored loudly overhead at the crack of
dawn, covering stories on the adjacent campus of the University of
California, Berkeley.

Some of what we vented about was unique to our experiences
living, studying, and ministering in the People's Republic of Berkeley, but much of it, we began to realize, was not, and was applicable
to students at other seminaries. Friends began asking to invite their
classmates who were studying at other schools and needed a place to
vent, commiserate, and seek advice. As years passed, not only were

classmates invited to join, but colleagues, as we finally began performing the sort of life-changing ministry that we had trained for years to do. From a late-night shenanigan that started almost as a joke between two roommates came a community of over two hundred and fifty ministers and seminarians who came to trusted colleagues for unbiased counsel, a fresh perspective, or simply a listening presence when the demands of our sacred vocations became too much.

Online groups like ours are taking on some of the tasks of traditional local ministerial associations, which are meant to provide clergy with much-needed spiritual connections in what can otherwise be very isolating work. Sometimes, these local associations produce strong and vibrant communities, but at other times, they can shut out ministers of a particular theological or political persuasion. In my own experience with local ministerial associations, comments made by colleagues—even seemingly offhand remarks—about liberalism, Islam, marriage equality, and other similar wedge issues created a stifling effect for me, a pastor whose theology is quite orthodox but whose political views were clearly outside of the association's established norms.

Politics is one thing, though. Basic sexual identity is another. For clergy—and laypeople, for that matter—who identify as LGBTQ, a local ministerial association may be an unwelcoming place not only on an ideological basis but also on a fundamentally human one. Online groups, especially private groups where invisibility can help protect confidentiality, have come to offer an alternative venue for clergy to safely seek out spiritual support from their colleagues. Those colleagues can be located anywhere. Our little Facebook group now claims members from a variety of time zones across both the United States and Canada. Despite the geographical distance, we feel safe enough to honestly and forthrightly share our struggles and concerns with the group from a place of tender, even intimate, vulnerability.

There is something Christlike in experiencing that level of trust, even if it takes place from behind a computer screen. After all, Christ ministered to his disciples on Maundy Thursday hidden from view, ensconced in the Upper Room in Jerusalem, breaking bread with them one last time. The intimacy of such moments is something millennials are able to find online as well as in person.

Access to the tools of social media represents a potentially seismic releveling of the playing field that has otherwise favored the traditionally exclusionary associations within the church. To go elsewhere for community is an act of spiritual survival, but it is also an act of spiritual resistance to strictures within the church that have excluded its children for too long. The creation of new ways to foster spiritual connection represents a significant departure in how millennials live in community from our elders, and harkens back to the seeking of new communities by pioneers who saw no life for themselves in the towns and cities they were from.

While it may not be the same as being able to catch up with your local group over coffee every month, online groups and forums can offer a profound experience of fellowship for all generations. Younger generations serve as pioneers for harnessing the connective power possible within such contexts, in part as a result of having been driven out of more traditional contexts where the reins of power still remain far beyond our collective grasp.

The Church of Facebook

In June 2017, Facebook founder Mark Zuckerberg caused a bit of a stir in Christian digital circles when he proclaimed that social media could and would one day fulfill the same basic functions of a church community, saying, in part, "It's so striking that for decades, membership in all kinds of groups has declined as much as one-quarter. That's a lot of people who now need to find a sense of purpose and support somewhere else. . . . People who go to church are more likely to volunteer and give to charity—not just because they're religious, but because they're part of a community."[7]

---

7. John Shinal, "Mark Zuckerberg: Facebook Can Play a Role That Churches and Little League Once Filled," *CNBC News*, *https://www.cnbc.com/2017/06/26/mark-zuckerberg-compares-facebook-to-church-little-league.html*, June 27, 2017, last accessed December 18, 2017.

Almost immediately, the responses went up—not just in Christian media publications like *Christianity Today* but also in secular media outlets like the *Guardian*—talking about how Facebook, and social media as a whole, could not possibly replace a physical congregation. The writers of those articles were not wrong—not entirely, anyway. Geographic proximity offers more than a shared local sports team or annoying, idiosyncratic traffic patterns; it offers people the opportunity for liberating emotional and spiritual connections. Text on a screen—or even a person's image and voice through Skype or FaceTime—cannot yet cover the breadth of communication in our unspoken body language and facial expressions.

That said, Zuckerberg may have been on to more than many gave him credit for at the time. Online technology is used for many forms of social interaction nowadays, from the striking up of otherwise impossible friendships to the formation of wholesale communities that bond together in profoundly moving ways. That is not to say that Zuckerberg was not overselling the impact and influence the grand shift his company has wrought on society. But for churches and Christian writers to reflexively dismiss his words as unrealistic actually proves his point: it may seem unrealistic from within our own bubbles, walled off from the shifting winds of popular culture. By bringing people into contact with each other outside of their traditional social circles, online communities offer one way beyond the bubbles that churches can easily become. If your daily or weekly routine is mostly limited to people within your church, that church has become a bubble that an online community can lead you out of. Outside of our bubbles, the idea of a social media congregation may not be so ludicrous. Those communities, in fact, already exist.

The blessing—and difficulty—for existing congregations is that these online communities are easily fostered at little financial expense. Set up a private Facebook group, invite people, and you can start building your own "We Say Fudge" community within minutes. The ease with which such infrastructure is available is the blessing. One of the main difficulties for sustaining an established church is in raising the funds for their programming and mission work. After all, the offering plates and the tithing boxes cannot easily be passed around online, can they? And would people even financially support an online congregation at the same level as they would a brick-and-mortar church?

The first question is addressed somewhat by e-commerce services that enable charitable giving online, but such services either charge the organization a subscription fee or take a service fee of 3 to 5 percent from the total donation. But there are workarounds. For many years I was able to donate the reward points I accumulated on one of my credit cards to any number of charitable organizations, and my bank covered the transaction fees so that 100 percent of the donation went to the organization. I used that service for years to donate to my alma maters as one of my spiritual disciplines. There should be no reason why churches could not encourage similar giving, whether the church has a visible online presence or not.

The second question is moot, as many traditional churches are not being financially supported at the levels they require. Since digital real estate is far less expensive than office space and a sanctuary, an online community would incur far fewer operating expenses—at least, aside from potential meetups or other in-person activities. Building community in ways which do not break the budgets of a cash-strapped generation will require creativity in new mediums that many neighborhood parishes may not be used to, or even distrust, but the potential alternative is for the church to miss out on being a source of spiritual nourishment for that generation altogether.

I am not saying that we are at the dawn of purely online churches with no physical presence to speak of. I am simply saying it is a direction full of interesting possibilities. Just as colleges and universities are moving towards hybrid models of facilitating classes in both physical and digital spaces, the church needs to also consider how we can live in both worlds and still foster community. Already, the regional Disciples of Christ office that governs my ministry credentials has moved to such a model, freeing up resources that used to pay rent and designating them for doing ministry instead.

Just as the meaningful friendships struck in the crucible of all-night cramming sessions and subpar cafeteria food are an indispensable part of a residential college or seminary experience, so too are they found amid the social media accounts of people who do not even share a time zone, much less an alma mater or a religious affiliation.

Will Tweet for Marriage or to Make Friends Across the Ocean

One of the most exciting moments in online friendship is getting to meet the person behind the Twitter account or the Instagram handle in person. It is the moment when you go from being "Facebook friends" to being friends and, at least for a short while, get to enjoy the benefits of geographic proximity.

The benefits of geographic proximity to the pioneers of the Oregon Trail were obvious—safety in numbers, the pooling of resources, and an array of different skillsets all contributed to how a wagon train might ultimately fare on the trail. But they were also brought together by a shared purpose, whether that purpose was the desire to get rich quick, like the forty-niner prospectors of the California gold rush, or to escape the violence of their environs, like the Mormons who settled in what is now Utah. That shared sense of purpose is what can bring people together in the online era of spirituality, just as much as geographic proximity can.

On top of getting to meet people I had only connected with online, I also have gotten to worship at their churches, sit down at the table with them, and be in the physical presence of their communities of origin. Our face-to-face connections began online, and often as a result of seeking one another out. Compare that to simply being put together at the same place and time through any manner of circumstance, such as a shared employer or school. Yet through mutual interests which prompt hashtags and shared status updates, new connections emerge more through purpose than shared geographic proximity—the twenty-first-century version of networking.

The growth of life-changing relationships online is not so revolutionary a notion in a day when people find spouses through online dating—myself included. In fact, online dating is an apt example of the phenomenon of which I speak: the intentional seeking of new relationships, friendships, and connections may well mushroom, purposefully or otherwise, into a community. My wife and I met through an online dating website, Chemistry.com, and through our array of now-mutual friends, we have created a new community for ourselves. I find joy and delight in her friends, as she does in mine, and we have a trail of mutual friends, if you will, who lay claim to our attentions equally from our seeking out one another.

These trails of relationships sometimes open up in unpredictable ways. While chapter seven will serve as a more in-depth discussion of the millennial generation's response to the revival of white nationalism, it is critical to remember that America's millennials are not the only young people facing down such a looming specter of hate and sinful thinking. It took an introduction via Twitter to a few remarkable people across the Atlantic Ocean for this millennial Christian pastor to take that lesson to heart.

In Germany, the Christian Democratic Union's Angela Merkel won a fourth term as chancellor in 2017, but it was a Pyrrhic victory, as the Nazi-esque *Alternative fur Deutschland* (AFD) Party became the first far-right party to win seats in the Bundestag. The AFD did not win just a few seats, either: it won eighty-seven, many of which came at the direct expense of Merkel's CDU, as both the CDU and its institutional partner, the Social Democratic Party (SPD), suffered substantial losses at the polls. In response to the unbearable political reality of a neo-Nazi party with seats in the Bundestag, Germans took to Twitter with the hashtag #87Prozent, which means "87 percent," the percentage of German voters who voted for a party other than the AFD.

I had seen firsthand the seriousness with which Germany takes both its past and present when I visited in 2004 as a part of a music and cultural exchange program through my high school.

George W. Bush had invaded Iraq the previous year over the vehement protestations of many European leaders, including Germany's then-chancellor, Gerhard Schröeder. The discussions I had about the war with the pair of German brothers in my host family were intense—not because I favored the war, but because the brothers were surprised to learn that I vehemently opposed it.

Additionally, Ronald Reagan had passed away just days earlier, and his funeral took place while I was in Germany. I watched it on television with my host family, and the tension was thicker than cement. Reagan had had a historic moment in Germany when he stood at the iconic Brandenburg Gate and demanded, "Mr. Gorbachev, tear down this wall," but his legacy was decidedly mixed at best, and my German family watched his funeral in pregnant silence, perhaps afraid of offending their American houseguest, even though I am so young that my entire experience of Reagan's second term was spent in diapers.

Those memories came flooding back as I read the #87Prozent tweets. Living in a country that goes out of its way to minimize its own crimes against humanity, my heart broke thinking of the shame Germans who were raised with the specter of Nazism in their country's relatively recent past must have felt. I took to my keyboard and hastily typed, "As one of the 54 percent of American voters who didn't vote for Trump—I see you, #87Prozent. I see you. I hear your voice. Danke." And I clicked that quill-and-parchment button that posts a tweet.

I did not expect anyone to reply, but several people did, with heartfelt sentiments echoing the same feelings of shame and encouragement. They came not just from Germany, but from Norway and the Netherlands as well, where the latter's own version of the AFD has risen under the guise of Geert Wilders and his Islamophobic *Partij voor de Vrijheid* ("Party for Freedom"). We each clicked that oblong "follow" button. I gained new acquaintances eight time zones away whose perspectives I now find invaluable in seeing areas of the world I otherwise would only see through the oft-distorted lenses of our media outlets that, erm, claim to be fair and balanced.

Connections like these represent a crucial component of many a millennial's need for community. The digital realm presents us with ample opportunities to create new communities and the means to both cultivate and maintain them. They are communities that have come about for a particular time and place, just as the wagon trains of pioneers once did. Increasingly, these communities become meaningful to us in ways that we could not have predicted. And for such serendipity, I find myself giving thanks.

Think of the apostle Paul, who was rarely able to personally visit the church communities that he served and, in many cases, helped to plant. Yet as he wrote to the Philippians and the Corinthians, the Romans and the Thessalonians, those communities remained close to his heart, even though he was hundreds of miles away. The consensus among most Bible scholars is that Paul had not visited the church in Rome when he wrote the Epistle to the Romans, yet he repeatedly professed his love for them and their leaders. He was a millennial before there were millennials, fashioning entire relationships out of nothing but a geographically distant—yet emotionally and spiritually close—connection. His letters were the best technology available to him to maintain the connections he had made across geographic and relational distances. Like millennials, Paul had to repeatedly explain to disbelieving temporal and spiritual leaders why his community of friends and fellow seekers was so far-flung. He had to repeatedly justify his ministry throughout the Acts of the Apostles and his letters. The church is better off for Paul having done so because of the glimpse his words offer us into the formation of some of the first communities of Jesus followers.

The intimacy Paul displays in his letters, and that all of us display to our friends and loved ones, is not found solely in face-to-face meetings. The stories we share online are as vivid, as personal, and as tender as any I have had shared with me in the confidence of a hospital room or my church office. And they deserve to be treated as such.

Online Confessionals

"I'm trying to find my way back to God, but for the life of me, I cannot see the road."

"He told me that I cannot be his friend because I am not Christian. I'd do anything to get that kid back. He's my best friend."

"I'm always left feeling a need to believe in God. But I don't. I haven't for many years."

Earlier in this chapter, I shared with you a few of the public responses to my Reddit AMA threads, and how they emotionally and spiritually affected me. But I also received private responses like those paraphrased above. They, too, are part of the connective power of online media. The sense of connection extends from the public sphere well into the private sphere—the world of emails, text messages, and direct messaging. While most clergy take coursework on how to provide pastoral care and counseling, the operating assumption tends to be that such care is given face-to-face, in personal settings, or at least over the telephone. We are less likely to be prepared to offer Christian care to one another in textual formats, but there are very real reasons why someone might choose to open up in a private online setting: the anxiety of a one-on-one encounter, especially if there are negative experiences with the church in the person's past, can add to the difficulty of finding a pastor or prayer partner who fits their needs in their local area.

In such circumstances, the ability to connect across time zones and even nations is a godsend in the truest sense of the term. The stories of the people paraphrased were such a godsend for me because I was able to learn some of the different ways people have experienced the Christianity I hold dear. Their willingness to put their trust in me as a stranger on the other end of a digital thread was trust that they may not have been willing to put into a Christian loved one or a clergyperson where they lived. While that may strike you as odd, I have found it to be an increasingly common theme in my relationships with friends online. That trust has become a

two-way street. I have grown to trust their opinions and advice as
they continue to trust in mine.

A quest for spiritual food in a digital wilderness necessitates at
least some vulnerability, especially if one elects to actively participate in online mediums that connect people to one another. Putting
yourself out there the first time you visit a physical church can be a
formidable experience, and this is equally true for online spiritual
communities. The importance of a person's search for a safe space
to be themselves, and to be spiritually nourished, remains the same
regardless of whether that search takes place online or in person.
The end goal is ultimately the same: to keep yourself from going
hungry along the trail.

Our private, intimate online connections create a space for
someone to be in a state of vulnerability and allows them to receive
pastoral care and Christian compassion. In the same way that lawyers include disclaimers in their email signatures that their commu-
nications may constitute privileged information, I have come to treat
such moments of providing care and counseling online as sacred,
privileged, confidential, and deeply meaningful to my sense of vocation as a Christian pastor who also happens to be a millennial.

Because such conversations are so sacred, it is right for
millennials—or any generation—to seek out a "safe space" of
family, friends, and allies, even if that safe space is an online
setting. Jesus sent his disciples out and instructed them to seek
out friends in their travels and ministries, and to bear witness
to when they were treated ill, saying in Luke 9:4–5, "Whatever
house you enter, remain there until you leave that place. Wherever
they don't welcome you, as you leave that city, shake the dust off
your feet as a witness against them."

The behavior of millennials to seek out people who will affirm
us is a part of that same trail laid out by Jesus and his disciples:
to remain in houses—both physical and virtual—where we know
that we will be safe as we venture outward into the world, intent on
making a difference. Nobody accused the disciples of needing "safe
spaces" when they sought homes that welcomed them. When we are

bullied, harassed, or abused online, we are fully prepared to shake the dust off our feet as we click the "block" and "report" buttons on our devices.

But good behavior, much less the sort of behavior that engenders the level of trust necessary to share the emotionally fraught aspects of our lives, is hardly the rule on social media.

When the Internet Snaps Back: Bullies, Trolls, and Broods of Vipers

"Looks like you should be more worried about your next Big Mac killing ya."
"You are a false teacher [and your] church spreads heresy."
"You are a snake . . . a viper . . . you do not represent Christ in any manner. You are a nobody."

These are just a few excerpts from some of the delightful "fan mail" I have received during my years of parish ministry—and these do not get into the truly scary stuff I have had to stare down, like threatening emails from "churches" classified by the Southern Poverty Law Center as hate groups that celebrate the murderous work of Christian domestic terrorists like Eric Rudolph and Scott Roeder. Yet I know that I present a much less prominent target than many of my peers. Were I female or LGBTQ, especially as an ordained pastor, or a person of color as opposed to simply a person of ethnicity, I would almost certainly be subject to a much steadier stream of such bile and invective from the trolls that tweet out from beneath their bridges on social media. This chapter on searching for spiritual fruit in the online spheres of Christianity would not be complete without a discussion of the darker side of those spheres, which enable toxic voices instead of offering nourishment.

The toxicity, in this case, is self-administered: fully one-third of millennial Americans admit to trolling others online.[8] While this is

---

8. Jake Gammon, "Over a Quarter of Americans Have Made Malicious Online Comments," *YouGov, https://today.yougov.com/news/2014/10/20/over-quarter-americans-admit-malicious-online-comm/,* October 20, 2014, last accessed December 19, 2017.

only slightly higher than the overall rate of 28 percent,[9] it is higher nonetheless—and higher especially for men, who contribute the lion's share of internet trolling. And perhaps most damning, from a generational standpoint, is that our trolling and vitriol comes from much of the same racial resentments that fuel our elders. While millennials are a more ethnically diverse cohort than previous American generations, those of us who identify as white are almost as apt as our parents and grandparents to pull the lever for Donald Trump for president based upon our "white vulnerability."[10]

So, fellow millennials, and especially white millennial men, this section of the chapter is directed squarely at us. We may have spent the past few chapters talking about our need for our older generations to see in us the ways in which our good gifts are different but still glorious to behold, but this is not one of those gifts. If we are going to be the generation that journeys in search of a new and better frontier, we must be eager to self-reflect and improve. Our faith and common humanity demand nothing less of us.

In the original *Oregon Trail* games, hunting took place with a small pixelated figure strolling around the screen and wildly shooting in every direction upon seeing a buffalo or a bear—or a rabbit or a squirrel, if you fancied yourself a good shot. You were not graded on accuracy. If you were like me, you did not care about overhunting, no matter how much the game warned you not to. Take that sort of gameplay and juxtapose it with how many of us are behaving online, wildly shooting at any target that pushes our buttons, regardless of the damage we might inflict. It is no way to interact with the world. It is no way to interact with humanity. But it is how we have come to respond to both. That must not be so.

In one of his most vitriolic public speeches, Jesus absolutely harangues the Temple authorities in Matthew 23 for their lack of

---

9 Ibid.

10. Matthew Fowler, Vladamir E. Medenica, and Cathy J. Cohen, "Why 41 Percent of White Millennials Voted for Trump," *Washington Post*, *https://www.washingtonpost.com/news /monkey-cage/wp/2017/12/15/racial-resentment-is-why-41-percent-of-white-millennials-voted -for-trump-in-2016/*, December 15, 2017, last accessed December 19, 2017.

regard for the poor and marginalized people in their spiritual care. Jesus hurls all manner of insults at the religious leaders, calling them hypocrites, whitewashed tombs, and broods of vipers. We have disregarded the core of Jesus's message concerning wrongdoing towards the outcast and marginalized and have replaced it with name-calling, almost regardless of the circumstances.

We have exposed ourselves as the real brood of vipers. We have shown ourselves to be the ones who would sooner puff ourselves up with the misfortune we inflict upon others rather than demonstrate any notion of divine calling to the identities, vocations, and roles that we hold in our lives. Growing up in our congregations as children, many of us saw how appallingly adults were capable of treating one another. Now millennials are reflecting that same behavior, in new ways and in new venues, as a part of the same cycle of pain and hurt that we as people and as Christians have inflicted on each other for generations. The good news is that this is also a cycle we are capable of breaking, should we take responsibility to do so.

Escaping the Cycle

James, the oldest of Jesus's brothers and one of the leaders and martyrs of the early church, writes extensively in the third chapter of the New Testament letter bearing his name about the urgent need for believers to tame their tongues. James notes that we bless and curse from that same speech, and those curses he compares to the widespread destruction of wildfires—a danger on the historic Oregon Trail and in the computer game. Words may not be sticks and stones, but they emotionally and spiritually maim, wound, and injure—even when only typed into a keyboard and displayed across a screen. The increased capacity of, and our comfort level with, online technology makes the scope of this problem unique to younger generations. We have tools with which to inflict harm that James could not have imagined in his time and space. Yet his warning has stood the test of time, and an honest acknowledgment of its truths is needed.

Millennials, we are capable of being so much more than the bogeymen we have fashioned ourselves into. In the hurting and wounded world that we are fast inheriting, we cannot afford to continue contributing to the injuries, and we cannot afford to ignore our calling to be a generation that points the way forward, not backward. We ought to be, as the omnipresent Mohandas Gandhi says, the change we wish to see in the world.

Faced with such a moral imperative, let us then pursue that calling to be better, to go high, to stride forward filled with the fruits of the "wisdom of above" that James describes: mercy, fairness, genuineness, and right action. Let us be that change.

And let us pursue that calling with passion worthy of that self-same wisdom of above.

From Bare-Bones Rations to Filling Portions

One surefire way in *Oregon Trail* to decimate your wagon party's health was to switch your rations over from "filling" or "meager" to "bare bones." Doing so conserved food, but at the deleterious expense of the wellbeing of your party members. It was a desperation tactic more than anything else—unless intended to see how quickly you could wipe out your entire party, which I must confess, as an elementary school student, I was not above attempting from time to time.

Millennials have been living off bare-bones spiritual rations in a variety of ways. We have been shut out from seats at the table in our brick-and-mortar churches, we have been turned off to religious education after the stifling experiences of many of our K–12 Christian schools, and all the while, we have been given largely unfeeling, uncaring, and unhelpful advice from our elders: "You just need to wait your turn." "Don't rock the boat so much." Where we have not been able to joyfully become a part of the fellowship of Christian community, we have sought our own—often outside the confines of the church as it currently exists, and often in the realms of social media, which constitutes a significant part of our frontier.

Our sojourn has not been without risk. Trolls, bullies, and misanthropes roam the digital landscape in full force. But such is the way with pioneers, souls who are willing to at least attempt to survive an untamed wilderness in order to build up new communities. When the former ways prove barren, we seek out new ones.

Like the pioneers of old, millennials endeavor to break free from this cycle of poor nourishment. And, like the pioneers of old, millennials have turned to some untamed and often vicious environs—in our case, social media and the internet—in which to construct for ourselves these new communities of the twenty-first century that spiritually feed us.

In many instances, we millennials have chosen to find spiritual nourishment and enrichment outside of the pews and Sunday school rooms of our elders. Rather than condemning us for a choice we did not make lightly, the church must do the work to understand our reasons. This work is critical if the church is to have a future with the millennial generation, whether that future is online, or in a traditional sanctuary, or some combination of the two.

Such an understanding is a big request to make of the church from a generation whose relationship with it remains complicated, but at a minimum, it represents a welcome shift from the current stagnation in so many quarters of the body of Christ.

We say every Easter that Christians are a resurrection people. Embracing the ways in which new generations seek that resurrection would be a welcome way for the church to boldly live out that worshipful proclamation of eternal life, as John 4:24 says, in spirit and in truth.

Chapter 5

Bartering and Bargaining
When and How to Repair Our Brokenness

"I'll leave you here for a moment and go make some phone calls. We can meet outside when you're ready."

My wife gets up to leave from the pew she and I had been sharing for several minutes in the chapel of the Providence Medical Center in the heart of Portland, Oregon.

We have just received the news at the hospital's diagnostic imaging department that the eleven-week-old baby she was carrying is no longer living. My wife will be scheduled within hours for surgery to remove the baby.

I sit alone in the pew silently for a while before glancing up at the crucified Jesus on display in the nave at the front of the chapel.

"Tell me what I have to do, and I will do it. This is the one thing I have tried to create for myself, after years of training and years of serving you. Why are you taking this away from me?"

Shaking, my voice grows more emphatic. The expletives begin to issue forth.

"I know taking out the punishment for the sins of the father on the newborn child is sort of your thing in scripture, but I wasn't expecting that from you now. I know I'm a snarky, gruff, irritated jackass of a servant, but it's not like I saw someone else's vineyard, killed them and took it for myself, and had a prophet tell me you will punish my child for it. Why are you doing this?"

I know I am but one of millions of potential fathers who have had their beloved experience a miscarriage. I do not care. Right now, misery doesn't want company—misery wants answers.

"*I've dedicated and baptized your children. I've watched them grow. I've married and buried them. You entrusted them to me. Why will you not entrust me with a child of my own?*"

I begin to realize I sound like many of my own pastoral charges across the years who have bitterly wept and confided in me their own doubts about God's love for them after a crisis or a disaster. And I have even fewer answers for myself than I do for my congregants.

"*I know this is not a quid pro quo; I don't get preferential treatment just because I'm your servant. Do I need to settle for not having this in my life? Do you need to hear me cry 'uncle'?*"

I close my eyes, feel the tears against my eyelids, and will myself to rise to my feet.

"*You know that I love you. You know that I'll always love you. But right now, enough with whatever wrath of yours this is that you're taking out on me. Enough. I'm through with it.*"

I leave the chapel. I see my wife on her phone and I walk over to her. She tells me that in addition to the phone calls, she has been sending out text messages, and that several of our friends are dropping everything for that day to be there for us.

I realize that God never really left us after all. I look at my wife and smile. I think of the times we have ministered to our friends who have suffered the same miscarriages and losses of life that we have, and I think of what Jesus taught: we reap what we sow. And God sows love.

We tell a close friend the news, and she replies that there will be fresh cookies waiting for us when we arrive home. We get in the car, call both sets of parents to break the news that they are temporarily furloughed from grandparent duty. To bolster us, more of our friends call during the drive home. None of these friends we contact immediately are "churched." But they are our church.

Our first evening as not-future parents takes place around our dinner table surrounded by friends who love us without reservation. They arrive as soon as they are able and stay late into the night, until they

know that we will be well—that, as the medieval prophet Julian of Nor-
wich wrote, ". . . all shall be well, and all shall be well, and all manner
of thing shall be well."
  It is a lot like church. Yet it is not quite church, either.
  It is what church has often been, but not to everyone; what it
could be, but is not yet to all: a place to repair the brokenness, heal the
wounds, and restore wholeness.

One of the most critical functions of a church is to provide emotional spiritual support the minute the fertilizer hits the proverbial
fan. While it may not be the primary gift of some congregations,
many others have the rapid response to a death, miscarriage, or
medical emergency down to a science: phone trees, casserole
deliveries, and a voluminous mountain of notes expressing heartfelt sympathy.

Just as millennials have adapted to the new frontier of forming religious communities online, so too have we adapted in forming church-like communities out of friends and family. Where our
elders used to rely on a church directory, we rely on a mass text message to our contacts list. And where people used to rely on a congregational care team or even just a few small group members, we rely
on an assorted collection of friends with no overarching structure
that functions similarly to a church yet is very much outside the
confines of organized religion.

Part of the beauty in this newfound life outside of the traditional church comes from the unstructured and untethered lives the
younger generations live relative to the older generations we discussed in chapters one and two. But many millennials exist outside
of the church in reaction to how the church has inflicted spiritual
and emotional pain, to the extent that the church is often not trusted
by a hurting soul. Healing from woundedness—or, at least, the creation of the support networks which help us to heal—has become a
largely do-it-yourself endeavor. That endeavor may not often involve
congregational structures because millennials, spiritually inclined or
otherwise, have found those structures to be irrelevant or unhelpful,

or because the church has pushed those millennials away for any number of reasons that we have already discussed.

Sometimes, the latter feeds directly into the former. And it demands a remedy.

Bare Souls and Empty Wagons

One of the categories of items available for purchase at Matt's General Store back in Independence, Missouri, was spare wagon parts: wheels, axles, and tongues. Purchase too many, and you could not put your limited funds to other critical uses along the way to Oregon. Purchase too few, and your wagon party could end up immobilized on the side of the trail and forced to barter with fellow emigrants for the parts you needed to resume your journey. It was a way for the game to either reward your calculated decision-making or cause you to rue the moment you chose to be the cash-strapped farmer instead of the carpenter or banker.

Once you had traded for the necessary wagon parts, you could continue along the trail, but the lost time often loomed large when added to other potential setbacks, like wagon party members dying of dysentery or having your wagon tip over and losing your foodstuffs during a river crossing. One setback alone might not keep you from reaching Oregon, but as they piled up, they easily could.

Being stranded without the supplies you needed to continue on the trail not only made the game less enjoyable, it served an important purpose. Long before any of us in the millennial generation got our driver's licenses, we knew what it meant to be running on empty, even if only virtually. The absence of any margin for error could make the game a real hair-raiser towards the end, if the game decreed that it was the perfect time for something to break down. "Like fish tragically caught in a net or like birds trapped in a snare, so are human beings caught in a time of tragedy that suddenly falls to them," wrote Qoheleth in Ecclesiastes 9:12. But he clearly was not referring to random-number generators that determined you would go from fit as a fiddle to dying of cholera overnight.

The lack of predictability in the *Oregon Trail* game was a teachable moment for us millennials. Despite our best-laid plans, anything could go awry at any second. When things break down for us in our adult lives rather than in a computer game, we may not always turn to the church in the same ways that our parents and grandparents did. Often it is because we have constructed our social lives almost entirely outside the territory of a local congregation. But sometimes, it is because the church itself is the root source of that brokenness that desperately cries out for urgent repairs.

Millennials who laid bare their souls to the church as children have subsequently abandoned it as a direct reaction to the church's poor stewardship of their souls. My generation has seen the church for what it far too often is: an empty wagon, bereft of the sorts of lifegiving and life-sustaining supplies necessary to make a trek as arduous as the one towards salvation.

Millennials have subsequently found other arenas in which to seek out the necessary spiritual and emotional supplies like affirmation, love, and unconditional inclusion. As I shared earlier, Carrie and I first met online, and online dating has become a frequent way for millennials to meet romantic partners. Between 2013 and 2016, the number of adults ages eighteen to twenty-four who used online dating nearly tripled.[1] Even if other avenues are used to find companionship, the way that online dating has elbowed its way into the mix has deemphasized other places to meet people, including church. With such networks at our fingertips that do not make such emotionally and spiritually stifling demands of who millennials are as children of God, it is little wonder that my generation sees no urgent need for the church. What need would you have of an institution that harmed you emotionally or spiritually if all the outlets for emotional and spiritual growth that it promised could be found elsewhere, and without the church's hidebound parochialism to boot?

---

1. Aaron Smith and Monica Anderson, "5 Facts About Online Dating," *Pew Research Center*, *http://www.pewresearch.org/fact-tank/2016/02/29/5-facts-about-online-dating/*, February 29, 2016, last accessed December 20, 2017.

On paper, the church remains unique because, while you could enroll in an online or college Bible class, or perform community service through Habitat for Humanity or another exemplary organization, doing such things in ways that are purposely worshipful sets the church apart from civic-minded organizations and institutions. Functionally, however, the church is seen less and less as an admirable cause to give one's time, mental energy, and concern to, which is evidence of the massive, self-inflicted wound on Christianity. In order to heal itself of this personally administered injury, the church must first learn how to heal its relationship with the people that it has harmed. And healing first requires a diagnosis.

The Dangers of Misdiagnosing

My most memorable Christmas was in 1992, when I was six years old. I remember it for a particular gift: I was given a diagnosis for an illness that had literally crippled me. As internal hemorrhages and juvenile arthritis ravaged my feet, ankles, legs, and knees, I became increasingly incapable of walking without extraordinary discomfort. Some days, the pain was so acute that my parents had to carry me down the stairs from my bedroom to the front door. Then my kidneys stopped functioning properly, and I started passing blood. I lived in dread of my own body as each trip to the bathroom became an agonizing experience.

My pediatrician and other doctors were not sure what was causing my symptoms. Initially, they were concerned it might be lupus, but what I had was something different: Henoch-Schoenlein purpura. That diagnosis was a gift for several reasons. It was not necessarily a chronic illness like lupus. Like chickenpox, it was something eminently more beatable for a young child (as opposed to being even more difficult for older children and adults). My chances of having a reoccurrence or developing advanced kidney disease were much lower than if I had contracted it years later. With the proper diagnosis in hand, my doctors were able to focus on containing my symptoms while waiting for the illness to abate and hoping that it did not relapse, which thankfully, it never did.

The correct diagnosis mattered—for my treatment, for my parents' peace of mind, and for me, young though I was at the time. If you have ever had to go to your doctor and have them not be able to pinpoint your illness, you understand the need to know exactly what is happening to your body, and the concern—or even fear—that can set in when you and your doctors do not know.

If the need to know exactly what is causing our pain is true with our physical selves, then why should it not be so with our spiritual selves? The pain our souls suffer comes from somewhere. Sometimes it can be self-inflicted when we are particularly harsh upon ourselves, but often it arrives externally, from the words and deeds of others. Recognizing where that pain comes from is important not just for the person who experiences that pain, but also for the person who inflicts it, as a prerequisite for any repentance and reconciliation.

The church ought to be far ahead of our nineteenth-century pioneer alter egos in this regard. Not only has medical science advanced dramatically since the mid-1800s, but so too has our understanding of the mind and soul. We have benefited from new developments in psychology, theology, biblical interpretation, and so much more, yet we continue to approach new generations with outdated paradigms. In the United States, having a broken wagon tongue or dying of dysentery are things of the past. We no longer need to plan for them. It is likewise time the church began purposefully leaving in the past some of its behavior towards younger generations.

There have been a great many explanations masquerading as diagnoses for the exodus of millennials from the institutional church, and the similar uptick in religiously unaffiliated adults. The stodgy worship music. The irrelevant sermons. The outdated social customs. All of these contain kernels of truth, but they are all minor symptoms compared to the more serious underlying cause: the church has cared more about its own preferences than the need to meet others where they are. As a result, those who would dare to grace the church with a new vision, or who simply wish for the church to widen its circle to include them, find doors slammed in their faces.

The simple, straightforward diagnosis is that the church has, throughout its history, harmed a lot of people, even as it has helped countless people as well. The more complicated question of how we can so confidently arrive at such a diagnosis is the heart of this chapter. Divide and conquer has long been a tactic of the institutional church, and while that tactic may have come at the tip of the sword in centuries past, watching the church today use people outside its norms as bogeymen is still as painful as ever.

Along with the divide-and-conquer mindset being deployed along the lines of national, ethnic, racial, or sexual identities, we are seeing it deployed regarding generational identity too. There is some overlap between all these identities. While all generations poll higher now than in years past on landmark causes like same-sex marriage and adoption rights, millennials started at a higher rate of belief in such causes, and still poll at higher rates than their generational elders.[2]

Nor is the pain inflicted by our elders upon the youth exclusive to the millennial generation, as dividing people into the desirable insiders and the undesirable others according to any number of ill-conceived criteria is a centuries-old tradition, and one that no Christian should have an interest in defending, regardless of generation. Yet still the church, time and again, defends the infliction of such spiritual, emotional, and even physical pain. If there is to be any healing, the church must be honest and truthful about diagnosing this collective illness. For within that illness lies one of the biggest reasons millennials no longer seek healing or wholeness within the church: we are entirely done with serving as another generation's scapegoat. The temptation to treat us as such is, like so many other temptations, something the church must be delivered from.

---

2. "Changing Attitudes on Gay Marriage: Public Opinion on Same-Sex Marriage," *Pew Research Center*, *http://www.pewforum.org/fact-sheet/changing-attitudes-on-gay-marriage/*, June 26, 2017, last accessed December 20, 2017.

Deliver Us from Evil

I memorized the Lord's Prayer at a very young age. My childhood congregation recited it every Sunday before we partook of Holy Communion. Even though I did not understand what each line meant, I could recite it before I learned how to write in cursive or to multiply and divide.

As a child, I imagined literally being delivered from evil, physically whisked away by Jesus from the presence of Satan or the Adversary, who was always an ominous, shadowy figure to me. (I also used to have nightmares of Jesus being crucified against the side of our garage, so I clearly was destined to end up a pastor.)

For many millennials, that evil to be delivered from has come from both inside and outside the church. Many delivered themselves from it by leaving the church, sometimes at great emotional and relational cost, because of the spiritual, mental, and emotional injuries either inflicted upon them, or that they witnessed being inflicted upon others.

Inflicting such severe injury, whether physical or spiritual, must be seen by the church as evil, yet it is we who are doing that inflicting. LGBTQ youth have been made homeless when their religious parents disown them. Pastors and visible Christians with wide-reaching platforms have denounced millennial-aged athletes as unpatriotic—or worse—for their nonviolent, justice-minded protests. And women watch as Christian politicians circle the wagons after on-the-record allegations of sexual assaults; these same politicians rely on support from Christian voters to attain office, whether for a Senate seat from Alabama or the White House itself. All of these factors have contributed to a current climate in which an exodus is taking place—only instead of the Israelites breaking out of Egypt, it is millennial Christians breaking out of the church.

Exoduses, whether of an enslaved ancient people, of pioneers driving their wagon trails across an overland trail to Oregon, or of a generation of alienated believers, have the capacity to easily become insular. There is a reason we refer to a community adopting a bunker mentality as "circling the wagons." It is extremely easy to adopt such a defensive posture to anything outside your wagon train, whatever it may be—a congregation, a denomination, a political identity, or more. The destructive irony of the church having done this is that it has produced an even larger crowd outside the circle of wagons that, far from clamoring to get in, is more comfortable in the exodus that has gathered in the wilderness.

Individually within that exodus, one of two scenarios will often play out: either a millennial raised in the church was personally injured and was shunned by their home church or left of their own volition, or they witnessed the damage being inflicted on their peers and realized that they could no longer in good conscience remain in the church. In both cases, the net result is the same: a young person disassociates themselves from the body of Christ. The resulting consequences are manifold. Even those who elect to remain in the church, or who dedicate themselves to the church in the form of ministry, may guard themselves from such injury through any number of precautions: cultivating networks of friends outside of their church, compartmentalizing their church within their emotional lives, keeping their church at arm's length from their personal life milestones, and more. It is not necessarily out of malice or wishing their church ill. Rather, it is a survival mechanism as old as humanity itself—avoidance of what can harm us, which is partly how Carrie and I ended up as a pastor and his wife reaching out to their no-longer-churched friends for love and support in the immediate aftermath of a miscarriage. Even though we learned that day that we would not be delivering the child we had hoped to, we were delivered from the immediate raw pain of loss, if only for a couple of hours, by friends who existed entirely outside our Christian and church-centric social circles.

In the depths of our despair and hurt, we could not have been more grateful.

Deep Calls to Deep

Even though I took a class on the Psalms in seminary, it was a ten-minute homily on the tenth anniversary of September 11 that revolutionized the way I read those songs to God compiled in the Hebrew Bible.

I was preaching at my childhood congregation, one week before my first Sunday at Longview FCC. I worked alongside McKinna, a childhood friend-turned-fellow-pastor. We were invited to take ten minutes each to preach in tandem on the tenth anniversary of the day that defined our generation in the same way that the assassination of John F. Kennedy defined our parents' generation. We composed our sermons simultaneously and shared them with each other before giving them side by side as adults who had been forged as children in the crucible of the same congregation.

I preached on one of my favorite passages on maintaining faith in God in the face of grief and fear—Habakkuk 3:16–19, which the prophet sings as a wonderfully rich paean to God's goodness despite his misgivings about God that begin the book: "LORD, how long will I call for help and you not listen? I cry out to you, 'Violence!' but you don't deliver us. Why do you show me injustice and look at anguish so that devastation and violence are before me?"

McKinna elected to preach on Psalm 42, which contains the refrain, "Deep calls to deep at the noise of your waterfalls; all your massive waves surged over me." Like Habakkuk 3, it is a song of praise in the midst of strife. Unlike Habakkuk, a prophet whose existential angst with God mirrored my own, the psalmist speaks not of treading upon great heights but of being enveloped by the deep—that same deep we talked about in chapter three that was a source of chaos, discord, and even death to the ancients. Yet in the depths of his separation from the world, the psalmist finds a way to thank God: "I will again give him thanks, my saving presence and my God."

The light bulb in my spirit—dulled though it may have been—switched on.

Deep calls to deep.

The depths of which the psalmist speaks include agonizing pain: "With my bones crushed, my foes make fun of me, constantly questioning me: 'Where is your God now?'" It is the sort of pain I think of when I recall and pray for all of my friends and generational peers who have left the church over being wounded by it, only for their churches to respond not with remorse, but with, as the psalmist describes, taunts and hurtful questions. Recall that chapter four illustrated the breadth to which millennials have gone to escape the ways of the institutional church. Here, a closer examination of my generation's woundedness and mistrust ought to uncover the *depth* to which we have gone to flee from organized Christianity's trappings.

It is difficult—if not impossible—to underscore the scope of that flight. The closest I have seen anyone come to assessing its magnitude correctly is the Christian ethicist David P. Gushee, who recently wrote in his moving memoir *Still Christian*: "*The more parochial and narrow the version of Christianity in a particular context, the more it produces rebellion.* In other words, fundamentalism always produces an allergic reaction, which expresses itself often in secularism and sometimes in the development of a more creative religious alternative"[3] (emphasis his).

The deeper the narrowness of Christianity, the deeper the flight from it is going to be. So, in another fashion, deep indeed calls to deep. The deeper the church retrenches itself into its own parochialism and narrow partisan and institutional interests, the deeper the flight away from it is going to be. Insularity, then, whether it comes in the form of an exclusionary church or a circled wagon train, is extremely easy for us to double down on, even when doing so inflicts further emotional and spiritual harm.

For all the critique of millennials living our lives at the level of the surface, those of us with a spiritual or religious bearing still crave the depth of authenticity, of a community that wants us for who we

---

3. David P. Gushee, *Still Christian: Following Jesus Out of American Evangelicalism* (Louisville: Westminster John Knox Press, 2017), 108.

are rather than for who they want us to be. Far too often, the latter represents congregations searching for younger carbon copies of themselves while the former represents something simultaneously new and fearfully and wonderfully made. The way forward from this dilemma involves not the glitz and flashiness of the twenty-first century, but the habits and spiritual teachings of the first century. The psalmist wrote a prayer to us from thousands of years in the past of the deep hope he finds in God amid his deep pain and despair. Our own prayers for deep hope can be what propel us forward along the trail.

Expanding Prayer

As I said earlier, I memorized the Lord's Prayer at a very young age. Fully understanding the context from whence the Lord's Prayer came, on the other hand, took me many years of religious studies. In the Gospel of Matthew, the Lord's Prayer is a part of Jesus's Sermon on the Mount—in fact, it is the very heart of the sermon, prefaced with his wish that we pray "not as the Gentiles do," by "pour[ing] out a flood of empty words," suggesting that such a spiritually vacuous means of prayer was relatively popular at the time among non-Israelites. In Luke 11:1, Jesus is asked by one of his disciples how to pray "just as John taught his disciples," and the implication is that Jesus's disciples do not already know how to satisfactorily do so.

Even after memorizing Jesus's recommended prayer, we still do not know how to pray, in large part because we tend to view prayer too narrowly, as something to do in church on Sunday mornings, or around the kitchen table before a meal, or at night before going to sleep.

Millennials, in my experience, see prayer as something to be lived, not something merely to be said. When prayer is uttered but not lived out in one's life, alarm bells go off in our heads. And in a world that has presented us with a paucity of resources and a church that has not always prayed for us as it ought, millennials have adapted by seeing our choices as a form of prayer.

We pray with our ballots.

We pray with our wallets.

We pray with our choice of media consumption.

And we pray, sometimes whether or not we are connected to a church. Millennials no longer need a church in order to pray, because how we live out our values is its own prayer.

How we demonstrate what we value shines through even in mundane activities, such as playing a video game like *Oregon Trail*. You must decide how to spend your money and what goods you most highly value—do you spend your limited funds on more food, or on more spare wagon parts? More sets of clothes or more oxen? And if you are caught without enough of one or the other and are forced to barter, how much are you willing to give up to obtain what you need?

One of my values is still that there is power in communal prayer, in being able to pray together. To expand the practice of communal prayer beyond the platitudes of Sunday morning and into the everyday tasks that assert our values is a redefinition of prayer that the church sorely needs. That redefinition of prayer can be a cornerstone for the work necessary to reclaim organized Christianity's worth in the eyes of a millennial generation—one that has come of age watching the church proclaim one thing in its public prayers and sermons and entirely another in its acts of institutional self-preservation and partisan interest. Those are not values espoused in the Lord's Prayer, yet they time and again have been the values espoused by the church.

Prayer is far too narrowly defined in the church. It must become more encompassing of what Christians do outside of those moments kneeling in the pew, sitting at the kitchen table before dinner, or getting ready for bed. Embracing moments of Christian witness, prophetic teaching, and public behavior as moments of prayer offers a fresh mindset for the church—and one that its younger generations are increasingly ready for and, in many cases, have already embraced.

Jesus expanded our understanding of prayer with the Lord's Prayer. But living, rather than simply saying, the Lord's Prayer must be understood as a prayer itself, and an expansion of how we see the Lord's Prayer function in our own spiritualities.

How to Purposefully Begin Healing

Being made well in the name of Jesus Christ is a common theme throughout the Gospels: lepers, people born blind, and even the dead are all beneficiaries of the healing ministry of Jesus.

It is high time the church and its wayward generation joined those ranks.

We can choose to go about this sacred task with purposefulness or haphazardness. In *Oregon Trail,* healing from illness and injury or repairing a broken wagon part was largely a function of randomness. You could increase your odds by being a particular occupation, but it was still the electronic equivalent of a dice roll whether you died of dysentery or got well. But ours is far too important a task to leave to mere chance. Both the church and the millennial generation owe it to themselves to be intentional in their interactions with each other.

What I share here should by no means be considered the only— or even the best—way to bring about such healing, but it is a start, and one that I have found to bring about deeper mutual respect between me as a Christian pastor and my religiously unattached generational peers. It represents a far greater faith in both God and my fellow children of God than simply trying to bargain out of this estrangement with a variety of quid pro quos ("If we just do X/offer Y/say Z, they'll come!"). It has added depth and profound meaning to many of the friendships outside the church that I have come to rely on in moments of grief and vulnerability, and it has borne fruit time and again.

The acknowledgment of a mistake is the starting point of any genuine repentance and reconciliation. Anything else is simply a form of denial, whether partial or absolute, and millennials, having been subjected to massive amounts of marketing and analysis of our tastes, can smell BS coming from miles away. We know when we are being lied to or misled. If the institutional church is unwilling or unable to acknowledge that its policies, culture, and politics have repelled millennials, then I might as well end this chapter now.

But I do not think that is the case. Or, rather, I do not think that should be the case. While my words for organized Christianity may be harsh, I still believe that our churches remain filled with good people who believe in fulfilling the Law and the Prophets as Jesus would have had them do: by loving God with all their heart, soul, and mind, and loving their neighbors as themselves (Matthew 22:40).

In saying that, I am expecting far more from the church than what is often expressed by its most visible figureheads, the televangelists and the cable pundits, who may know how to get their words on the air but would not know the declaration from Jesus that the last be first and the first be last if it walked up to them and shook their hand. It is right to expect more from the church than that. If I did not have faith in the church, I would not be here.

The church must acknowledge that it has done wrong, and in some cases committed sin, by its children. Recognizing the church's history of subsuming the gospel into partisan politics is a part of that repentance. Another part is understanding that homophobia within the church has led to outsized numbers of homeless LGBTQ youth, higher rates of LGBTQ youth suicides, and an absence of feeling safe and welcome within the church for LGBTQ people. So too is a long-overdue affirmation from the church, especially its conservative branches, of women in positions of church leadership, including the position of pastor. The racial segregation of the church has scarcely improved since Martin Luther King Jr. famously remarked that the most segregated hour in the United States was eleven o'clock on Sunday mornings. And broadly excluding millennials, and Generation Z behind us, from the tables where decisions are made has led to the current crisis in the church. It is the crisis of an increasingly shallow pool for congregations and denominations to draw upon for positions of leadership, at a time when such visionary leadership is critical to undo the damage of the church's sins and errors.

These examples of wrong and sin to acknowledge are precisely that—examples. The list is by no means exhaustive. There is a lot for which the church needs to repent, even if we ourselves do not feel that we individually caused any of it. All of us in the church have a vital role to play in any future reconciliation.

From the acknowledgment of such sins, in my experience, come the softening of hearts and a genuine recognition that there are Christians working to right the wrongs of our faith institutions. Acknowledgment brings about acknowledgment in return.

The softening of hearts should not be seen as an automatic avenue into evangelism pitches—that, too, can often be part of the problem rather than part of the solution. But, as Jesus taught in Mark 4:26–34, the kingdom of God can grow from something as small as a mustard seed. An acknowledgment of the ways the church has hurt a conversation partner may feel almost painfully small, yet it is capable of powerful things in establishing a relationship built on respect between people who would otherwise regard one another with suspicion.

But most of all, trust is something that has to be regained day by day, month by month, year by year. That reality alone is enough for us to realize that there are no quick fixes, no easy answers, and no immediate turnarounds any more than there was a convenient exit ramp off the Oregon Trail. The trail before us is time plus effort, yet many congregations feel (or fear) that they do not have enough of either left in store. Whatever reserves remain in the rapidly aging pews—of mainline and evangelical congregations alike—may scarcely seem enough.

But they need to be. The acknowledgment of sins and the building of mutual respect between churches and the millennial generation, as I said, may not represent the only way forward, but it has represented the most consistently fruitful path in my near-decade of ministry as a millennial pastor. And that near-decade of experience is a trove that I trust.

Forward in Courageous Vulnerability

How does the church move forward post-acknowledgment of those sins? Millennials have already moved on, either with or without the church. Many millennials who have left are too hurt to come back on anything but their own terms, if they ever come back at all, and many more have grown tired of waiting on the church to stop catering to an overly idealized vision of the 1950s that never existed. The expectation that millennials be props in the church's pursuit of its glory days, like a kid whose stage parent tries to live vicariously through them, adds to the harm that such a one-sided relationship engenders.

The desire to return to a falsely idyllic era tends to manifest itself as an implicit bargaining process—if only we do this or that, we will be rewarded with the church of our past. That sort of bargaining may be fine when it comes to replenishing a wagon party's stock of spare axles and wheels, but not when it comes to replenishing a church's stock of trust and goodwill with its young people.

Instead of looking backwards, the church can join the millennial generation in striding forward. Yes, the future is uncertain, and it may even look bleak to many congregations. Yes, the hopes and fears piled up over all the years can be an awfully strong paralytic. But I have learned that engaging the future instead of running from it is an act of courageous and necessary vulnerability.

The day of our miscarriage, Carrie and I could barely process what was going on. But the day after was, in many ways, the first day of the hardest part of the whole ordeal. The truth had sunk in: our child was dead. We went from soon-to-be parents to yet another millennial couple that gets criticized for putting off parenthood. I remember seeing such articles show up in my social feed and literally shaking out of anger, pain, and sorrow. I remember the utter doubt that seeped over me, sometimes for hours at a time, as I sat alone, wondering if this meant we were not fated to be parents. And I remember the crushing bouts of grief that came at Carrie and me like tidal waves.

I did not let my church in on most of that grief. I could not. Not just because I was a pastor unable to put his own grief on his congregants, but because even if I had not been a pastor, I still was not sure of how safely I could let much of outside Christianity into my own mourning.

It was easy for me to feel stuck—as easy, I am sure, as it is for congregations to feel they are stuck, unable or unwilling to plunge forth along the trail that God has unfolded before them. That is why the image of being at a standstill on the Oregon Trail without the parts needed to journey onward keeps coming back to me. We have all been there at some point along our own trails. We (myself included) may well yet end up there again before our time on those trails is through.

Until such a time, I know now that it is incumbent upon each of us to bear one another's loads, just as the wagons and teams of oxen bore the loads of families seeking a new life for themselves. Such burdens are seldom light, or even comfortable, but they remain holy and sacred nonetheless. To help carry them until spare reserves of emotional and spiritual energy can be found and drawn upon is a divine honor.

If that is what is required of us to usher one another home, I can think of no better way to use what spiritual reserves we have remaining within us. And I can scarcely begin to imagine what a wondrous and glorious home it will be.

Chapter 6

Rafting the Columbia River
Handing Over Control to New Generations

The professor at the whiteboard rapidly unpacks his lecture on how to more effectively teach habits of giving of oneself generously—and not just financially—across the entire calendar and liturgical year. His material is based in part on use of the Revised Common Lectionary, a repeating three-year series of scriptural passages that many of my colleagues use in their own preaching: He is an engaging presence, so most of the seats in the convention center classroom are already full. I squeeze into a seat towards the back.

When he wraps up his lecture and explains what the next day will be in our continuing education learning sequence—a panel of different pastors on preaching stewardship in conversation with the lecture he just finished—he opens the floor for questions.

I raise my hand, like the overeager, still-sort-of-fresh-out-of-seminary pastor that I am. I am intending to not be a lectionary preacher. It is not that I dislike the lectionary, but it has never gotten the best preaching out of me, so I jettisoned it early in my career. I ask my question.

"What would be a way to utilize this material for those of us who are more thematic or sermon series preachers, or who don't regularly preach from the lectionary?"

His response is—and I am paraphrasing here—"You are doing it wrong. Just preach from the lectionary." Except he is even more curt and dismissive. Think of Professor Severus Snape from Harry Potter *and you get the idea. I almost expect to have points deducted from Ravenclaw for posing such an impertinent and unwelcome question.*

I am absolutely tongue-tied, dumbfounded that in front of an entire classroom packed with colleagues, I would be scolded by someone who knew nothing about me or my ministry because I did not make use of a sacred cow—a sacred cow that undoubtedly has genuine value, but one that did not birth the art and craft of preaching.

As a colleague I respect told me afterwards on Facebook, "The irony is that once upon a time, lectionary use by preachers was considered taboo. The pendulum continues to swing . . ."

Therein lies the crux of my dilemma. When we confer eternal value upon something that only came to prominence with our generation, we create the sort of graven images that God not only warns about, but expressly forbids in the Ten Commandments. There was a time when the church did not set its clock by the lectionary texts. There was a time when worship music came from something other than a pipe organ. There was a time when the church was not "our church."

I resolve in that moment, like an angry teenager who has been grounded and swears to never, ever become their parents, not to cultivate my own sacred cows as a pastor.

But I know better. And I know myself. I am going to need help to keep my resolution.

When commiserating with ministry colleagues over the difficulty of finding volunteers for church jobs, I sometimes joke that despite many churches being flag-waving, patriotic hymn-singing, America-celebrating enclaves of capitalist Jesus worship, we tend to run our churches a bit like a communist government's planned economy. In church, the number of jobs available and their descriptions are often determined by a central committee (a board of directors, a diaconate, a vestry, whatever it might be called in your congregation), and the nominating committee or the volunteer coordinator then goes off in search not of talented people to create jobs for, but people willing to serve the jobs that were created for them to fill. Aptitude, talent, and giftedness often play second fiddle to willingness—any willingness at all, sometimes—to do the job exactly as described.

This culture of static job descriptions and rote expectations lends itself to atrophy because there is no room for growth—only execution—and no room for fluidity or creativity—only automation. It is natural, then, that the more dynamic ways of the millennial generation would eventually clash with the more habitual methods of the church.

What this lecturer's words communicated to me was that giftedness for the task of preaching came secondary to *preaching in the manner to which the church has become accustomed.* Alliterated three-point sermons based on the Revised Common Lectionary that are neither too short or too long, neither too funny or too serious, with each of the three points containing one—and only one—illustration, are just some of the many arbitrary guidelines I see practiced as though Jesus delivered the Sermon on the Mount with the same sensibilities in mind.

What happens when you discover a talented individual who may well be gifted for the task being asked of them, but not in performing that task exactly as their predecessors did for decades? Even if some jobs within the church will likely always be the same (there will always be a need for people to teach the scriptures, to care for the sick, and to organize mission efforts), how those jobs will be performed going into the future will not remain the same, no matter how much we might want them to.

If I have given you nothing else in the previous chapters, I hope I have given you a snapshot of a generation that, whatever its spiritual scars, has prepared—and even braced—itself to navigate the slippery landscape of change that lies ahead. Like Moses in his forty years of exile, we are a generation prepared to survive on our own until God calls us forth with something great and good to do. Like the pioneers, we have chosen to make our homes elsewhere for the time being. My prayer is that my generation's exile from organized Christianity does not last quite so long. I, like Moses, will be an old man forty years from now. In order to shorten that span in exile, the church must be willing to travel down the trail, in the wilderness alongside the young people who feel forsaken, which means that it is time to cross another river together.

Raft the River, or Take the Toll Road?

Near the very end of a game of *Oregon Trail*, the player faces a critical decision: do you arrive in the Willamette Valley by way of the Barlow Toll Road, or do you raft the Columbia River westward? The former was more predictable, but expensive—especially if you had already burned through your cash reserves. The latter, in addition to being free of charge, gave you a chance to play something resembling a traditional video game for at least a fleeting minute or two as you daringly navigated your wagon down the river, dodging rocks, outcroppings, and other obstacles until you reached the landing in Oregon.

The choice, at least among my friends, was obvious. Only cowards took the toll road. If you cared about arriving in Oregon in style, you rafted the river. When it came your turn, your friends would drop what they were doing to gather around the computer and watch. If you were successful, you closed out your game knowing, as Virgil famously wrote in the *Aeneid*, that fortune indeed favors the bold.

In church governance, though, boldness is seldom favored. Congregations certainly talk a good game, with vision-casting, emergent jargon, and mission statements aplenty, but most of us in the church know that the structure that is around this year will be around the next year too, and likely the year after as well. What may have begun as a bold idea becomes a toll road of sorts, existing not for innovative ways of doing ministry, but as a route of least resistance, as the Barlow Toll Road exists for *Oregon Trail* players uninterested in rafting the Columbia River.

Continuity is given great deference in parish ministry, and I wholeheartedly include myself in that paradigm. Throwing the baby out with the bathwater was not my approach for the seven years I was in Longview, in part because I knew that I was the change. All of my predecessors had been middle-aged or close to it; I was only in my mid-twenties when I arrived. I knew what a leap of faith it was for the congregation to call me, and a combination of my deference to that reality and a dawning realization that there was so much more to congregational ministry than what I had been taught in seminary made me move forward initially with an abundance of caution. In truth, I probably could have moved more quickly while still honoring the history of what the Holy Spirit had accomplished in Longview long before I had arrived.

That need to strive forward, to make the choice to raft the river rather than take the toll road, has been encapsulated for me in a couple of profound instances. One was at a denominational conference I attended while in seminary, where a presenter compared his neighborhood church to his neighborhood grocery store. Over the years, he observed the store making constant changes to the products it offered and how those products were presented. Meanwhile, his church consistently refused to make any such changes to its programs and worship style.

It is not as though church is more timeless than groceries. Humans have needed physical food for as long as we have needed spiritual food. Jesus was tempted by Satan in the wilderness to turn stones into bread, and later used bread to represent his body at the Last Supper. As long as there is a market for the milk and honey of scripture, there will be a market for actual milk and honey as well. Yet the physical food is delivered by people more attuned to the current needs of families and households than those delivering eternal sustenance.

If grocery stores were run like churches, I think we would see far more of them go out of business. And in the sports industry, where traditional thinking held sway for decades, many teams ran themselves like churches until a particular book, Michael Lewis's *Moneyball*, became an invitation to a revolution of progress. It represented another way to take the trail, rather than relying only upon a river or a toll road. And one of the actors in the movie, based on the book that preached a parting call to embrace new ways of thinking, happens to hail, like the Oregon Trail itself, from Independence, Missouri.

The Church of *Moneyball*

The metropolitan area of my hometown of Kansas City has produced a remarkable array of acting talent. Comedic actors Paul Rudd, Ellie Kemper, and Eric Stonestreet all call Kansas City their birthplace, as do the legendary Ed Asner and *Saturday Night Live* alums Jason Sudeikis and Rob Riggle, the latter having attended my high school in Overland Park. Nor is Kansas City any slouch in the dramatic acting department: Janelle Monae, Dianne Wiest, and Chris Cooper, among others, all boast Kansas City roots. It is another character actor from the Kansas City area, however, who made the most outsized imprint on my memory: Arliss Howard. You may know Howard as Cowboy from Stanley Kubrick's iconic Vietnam War–inspired film *Full Metal Jacket*, but that film was before my time. I first saw Howard as the creepily sinister John C. Calhoun in Stephen Spielberg's 1997 film *Amistad*, about Africans who were kidnapped and sold into chattel slavery and then rebelled against their enslavers. Years later, Howard made a cameo appearance in the Academy Award–winning 2011 film adaptation of *Moneyball* as John W. Henry, the owner of the Boston Red Sox.

Henry bought the club in February 2002. Later that year he asked Billy Beane, the general manager of the Oakland A's, to be the general manager of the Red Sox, on the basis of the changes Beane had made in the way the A's evaluated its players to compensate for their extreme financial limits that put them at a distinct disadvantage. Henry so valued Beane's new and (at the time) unappreciated way of assembling Oakland's roster that he offered him $12.5 million over five years, which would have made Beane the highest-paid general manager at the time in the United States—in any sport. He makes the offer towards the end of *Moneyball*, and delivers a passionate soliloquy on the need for baseball to change, saying:

> It's the threat of not just the way of doing business, but in their minds it's threatening the game. But really what it's threatening is their livelihoods, it's threatening their jobs, it's threatening the way that they do things. And every time that happens, whether it's the government or a way of doing business or whatever it is, the people are holding the reins, have their hands on the switch. They go bat**** crazy.[1]

"Or whatever it is" is the operative phrase. The church is neither the government nor a business, although there are certain aspects of both that overlap. The church is its own organic being, wondrous and complex, and the phenomenon Howard, as Henry, describes is true for churches as surely as it is for governments and sports clubs: when the way of always doing things is threatened, the people in charge of doing those things often respond in profoundly negative ways.

His message of revolutionary change is not unlike the voices of those pioneers who gathered in Independence long ago to undertake together, for better and for worse, an endeavor that would forever change the country. How and why such changes take place have consequences that can outlive us. Our rich tradition of Christian ministry and teaching should not be thrown overboard when rafting the river. The mission at hand for millennial Christians within religious communities is to respect that history without worshiping it, and to usher our communities into their new futures across new rivers. The mission for congregations, in turn, is to avoid the sort of caution that makes the toll road overly appealing and transforms traditions into idol worship, and to make room for such rebirth, lest our churches become little more than time capsules.

---

1. "Moneyball (2011) Quotes," IMDB.com, *https://www.imdb.com/title/ tt1210166/ quotes /?tab=qt&ref_=tt_trv_qu*, last accessed February 20, 2018.

Time Capsule Churches (Or, Some Profound Thoughts on Shag Carpet)

A few years ago, I was talking with Wendy, a congregant who served as our wedding coordinator, about how best to take advantage of a rarely used second-floor room in our church building for our upcoming autumn programs. Standing in the room, she noticed that the carpet had begun to peel at its corners. This was not just any carpet, mind you. It was wall-to-wall, thick shag carpet, surely from the 1970s or 80s, and in the most putrid shade of green that I had ever seen. I remain convinced that nature is incapable of fully replicating that particular shade of green. It was genuinely a wonder to behold, and I say that as someone who grew up with plenty of shag carpet in his childhood home that was constructed in—wait for it—1978.

On a whim, Wendy and I decided to roll back some more of the carpet to see what was beneath it. Our church building was on the National Register of Historic Places, and its original brickwork and woodwork were awe-inspiring. Underneath this artifact from the disco era was the original hardwood flooring, in need of a new coat of polish but still beautiful.

To me, that room was a time capsule, a shell crafted for one purpose, but eventually stuffed with relics from a particular era, waiting to be discovered by subsequent generations. The shag carpet covered up the innate beauty of the room and its possibilities.

Wendy and I rolled up the rest of the carpet and disposed of it—without asking permission. I am grateful we did, because congregations, and even the wider church as a whole, too often look for reasons not to do something that will launch them across the river. A board member will object to the change. A donor will suggest that now is not the time for the change. Someone will make sure it gets back to the pastor that "some people have been saying," which allows an anonymous contingent to exercise control.

None of these reflexes towards toll road–esque continuity entice millennials into positions of leadership. Much of the time, they have the opposite effect, and actively repel young Christians from seeking positions of congregational leadership once they see how unseriously they are regarded when they suggest timely changes to those traditions or that those traditions might best be eased into retirement. Congregations continue in a position of stasis because they will not roll up the shag carpet, and millennials hear the message that the congregation is not interested in their leadership. Millennials then fall back or withdraw, because that is what a fluid culture does in the face of a static culture: it finds another way.

How often have we, as the church, striven to cover up our innate beauty? The shag carpeting of a congregation's unspoken norms can stifle the spiritual growth of young newcomers. Such unspoken norms may have begun as necessary or even appealing when first instituted, but they now act as inhibitions to envisioning something fresh and new. When we in the pews are wedded to a version of church that has become a time capsule of our faith, we cling to familiar habits rather than doing the work to uncover the traditions that give us a solid raft to travel upon down the river of change.

Like the carpet that blanketed my parish's upper room, those habits must eventually be rolled up and discarded. And like the beautiful hardwood floor beneath it, the possibilities that are uncovered by reconnecting to the spirit of our faith that beckons us away from the toll road as a time capsule church will often astound us.

The next step is to raft the river instead of retracing the deep wheel ruts of the wagon trains that came before. Recognizing all of the factors that we have discussed so far—the changing economic, social, digital, and emotional realities that have shaped millennials' spiritual realities—can empower the church to say "yes" to ministering in a twenty-first-century world, rather than cleaving to a world that covers over both the power of our traditions and the possibilities for our future.

Leading by Yes, Not by No (Or Worse, "We'll Pray About It")

As we have discussed, congregational bodies of authority sometimes have the propensity to reflexively say "no" to any rocking of
the status quo that goes beyond a gentle sway. The programs that
ended before summer vacation will pick up in the autumn as they
have always done. The hymns that were sung several weeks ago will
be sung again exactly the same way. The Sundays outside of Lent,
Advent, Christmas, and Easter become increasingly interchangeable.

The expectation of familiar repetition along the toll road route
of church life unnecessarily increases the difficulty for congregations
to embrace constructive changes as the world changes around them.
Too often, our congregations stand in the midst of the maelstrom,
firmly planting their feet in the ground of their familiar habits.
They echo Martin Luther's famous words, "Here I stand; I can do
no other!" Yet instead of following the trail blazed by a renegade
monk who challenged the church's traditional practice of purchasing
indulgences, the church digs in over what color the covers of the
new hymnals should be.

Millennials look at such a dilemma and ask, "Do we even need
to purchase new hymnals? They're so expensive, and the church
already has a projector. Can we put the music up on that instead
and use the money for our outreach or mission ministries?"

The responses are often so familiar that they have become clichés:
"We don't know how people will react to such a change. . . . We
cannot expect everyone to just go along with it. . . . This is just the
way we've always done things." Such refrains have become idols on
whose altars innumerable revolutionary, visionary, and mission-oriented ideas have been sacrificed. Ideas that could lead congregations
into renaissance and revitalization. Ideas that bear the rich spiritual
fruit the church longs for. Ideas that can help us raft the river and
change the world.

The "no" to those ideas is not always immediate. It can be
strung out, begun with a "Let's pray about it," a phrase often said

in earnest, but that also serves as a preamble to the inevitable "no." By stringing it out, a congregation not only runs counter to Jesus's command in the Sermon on the Mount in Matthew 5:37 to "let your *yes* mean yes and your *no* mean no," but also gives potential false hope to young leaders in the making who desire to do ministry that builds the realm of God and speaks the gospel, but whom their congregation continues to keep at arm's length in deference to the ruts upon the toll road. As a spiritual community predicated upon saying an emphatic "yes" to God as revealed in Jesus Christ, we remain overly dependent on the word "no" as a means of quashing adaptation.

Millennial Christians are ready to lead the church, but the question remains: is the church ready for our leadership?

Exile and Estrangement

Millennials feel exiled from the church and its positions of influence and mission, which has led to us forming our own wagon trains and communities. The church, meanwhile, feels increasingly exiled from American culture, having lost the lofty and relevant perch it previously occupied. There is plenty of discussion recently spurred by conservative Christian author Rod Dreher's book, *The Benedict Option*, concerning whether the church should deliberately choose exile, but the more pressing reality is that the church has mostly been the one doing the exiling of a great many people whom it has hurt.

The church, therefore, has contributed to its own sense of exile by estranging some of its own. Such estrangements over religion are hardly new, whether it is a fundamentalist pair of parents disowning their LGBTQ child or a member of a cult-of-personality congregation like the former Mars Hill Church being instructed to shun a friend and neighbor. The consequences of years of such estrangements are catching up to the church, and as it holds ever tighter to the cultural twins of nostalgia and ethically flexible but ideologically rigid politics, the feelings of estrangement and exile become increasingly profound. The exodus of people on the trails leading away from the church is populated both by those who have left of their own volition and those who have been forced into exile.

I use the term "exile" here partly for its biblical connotations. The Babylonian exile was one of the most traumatic events of the Hebrew Bible. Entire prophetic books were written around it. More than five hundred years afterwards, it was used in the New Testament as a point of comparison for Israel's treatment under Roman occupation. Exile is a form of collective trauma, while estrangement is more a form of personal trauma.

The millennial generation and the church are both in a state of spiritual exile, and that acknowledgment may offer both my generation and my church a new start down the Columbia River together. If, instead of each wishing a pox upon the other's house and walking away in opposite directions, each sought to bless the other, there might yet be room for reconciliation.

Living in exile is not the default state of being for either demographic. The church, especially the white American Protestant church, has long been accustomed to sitting at the epicenter of the country's civic religion, and millennials are increasingly comfortable with flexing our own cultural and civic muscles. But the existence of both millennials and the church in the public square need not feel like relatives who know not to push one another's political buttons when they meet over Thanksgiving dinner.

At my home growing up, the kitchen table became the children's table on holidays when our extended family came to visit, while the adults sat together in the dining room to talk about whatever boring subjects adults talk about. (It is still a mystery to me.) As the eldest child in my generation, I began agitating to be included at the adult table long before my sister and cousins, only to be rebuffed time and again by my parents, who I am sure simply wanted a break from me and my teenaged existential angst.

It is one thing to make that rebuff when the child is still a minor. It is another when the child is no longer a child, but an adult who is both able and willing to contribute constructively. For far too long, the church has sidelined the voices of Generation X and millennial members, except to use such voices in token roles to create a veneer of generational diversity. Just as the church should shy away from using its people of color, women, and LGBTQ people as window dressing, so too should it avoid treating its still-underrepresented ranks of the young in the same way.

The church table has been set, then, but it has resolutely kept new conversation partners rising from the ranks of adolescence at arm's length. This is partly due to the disregard older generations have shown toward their young. But it is also due to different paradigms of leadership between the older generations and the youth they have striven to keep away from the table until now.

The Committee to End Committees

My father-in-law, Bill, is a Southern Baptist lay leader who has spent his adult life performing remarkable ministries in his community. He currently heads up a project that involves constructing apartments for homeless women and children, and I hope the ministry I do in my retirement is even a fraction as amazing as his. He is also a skilled bureaucrat with a fine attention to detail that makes him a natural church administrator. His natural gifts led to his being invited by his home church to sit on a committee tasked with auditing all of the congregation's committees and proposing the elimination of redundant functions—or even, if need be, the elimination of entire committees. In other words, in hopes of having fewer committees around the parish, his congregation created . . . another committee. The punchlines practically write themselves.

Committee-based leadership is a corporation-centric paradigm of leadership, one that relies heavily on borrowed cultural behaviors and norms from the business world. While the church is not a for-profit company, and should not be run like one, certain principles of business leadership can translate into congregational life and leadership. However, as millennials are shut out of corporate leadership or start their own businesses with their own definitive cultures, the committee-based model is increasingly outmoded for a couple of reasons, both inside and outside the church's governing structures. Inside the church, concern is often given to ensuring that differing constituencies have a seat at the table when important decisions are being made. However, constituencies change in churches over time, as in almost any community, and what begins as a well-intentioned attempt to ensure parity can become an ossified gate through which newer Christians are not permitted to pass.

Here is where the second reason, from outside the church, comes into play: owing to the reasons we have discussed thus far, millennials' lives are far more fluid than those of our elders. The ad hoc nature of our lives extends interpersonally to positions of leadership and influence, where we are more willing to rotate roles in which we serve, and to rotate those roles with greater frequency.

An example from my ministry experience was when we expanded our small group network at Longview FCC to accommodate our growing number of young families. We added a group specifically for young women in addition to the women's and men's groups already in existence. The older women whose small groups had been functioning within the congregation for decades gave the younger women a wealth of instruction and advice on what to name the group and how to structure it. The younger women elected to follow some of the advice, but they also chose to blaze their own path, particularly in how to structure their leadership roles. They did not need a standard-issue, corporation-influenced hierarchy, but a more fluid and collaborative leadership model that focused on social connection and mission. The leadership roles they created for their small group reflected that shared need for relationship rather than hierarchy.

The fruits of their group's more collaborative, mission-oriented approach were tangible and lasting: that group started a fall festival from scratch that raised hundreds of dollars for various missions of the church, and their blueprint was later used by the entire congregation when the elementary school in our neighborhood lacked the volunteer resources to put on their spring carnival like other schools in the district. With the help of a couple of neighboring churches, FCC hosted the carnival for the school, using many of the same plans, resources, and ideas our young women's group had developed for the fall festival.

It was not radical by any means. We were not setting out to reinvent the wheel when we expanded our small group system. But by playing to their strengths and focusing on what they felt God calling them to do, the young women in Longview made a lasting imprint on how their congregation went about community outreach, which had a ripple effect throughout the parish to our neighbors at the school. By embracing the spiritual fruits of our young women as something to emulate, FCC expanded our mission and presence in our community in new ways.

Because the congregation's next generation elected to raft the Columbia River, even though their predecessors had grown used to the toll road, they demonstrated to the rest of the church that rafting was more exciting and allowed for adaptation to the challenges the work of being church presents. The established path of the toll road offers some certainty and continuity, and both routes ultimately arrive at the same destination: the Willamette Valley. Any approach to doing and being church should take Jesus followers to the same destination: God's grace and the promise of heaven. If the spiritual toll demanded by the trail is too expensive and exacting, the church should take to the river, even if the short-term risks seem higher.

Landing on Solid Ground

I cannot imagine the preaching professor who made an example of me for not utilizing the lectionary intended to do so, but he unmoored me as a young pastor with his answer to my question. The next day, I thought of little else. I felt humiliated to the point of questioning my own call to ministry. Those twenty-four hours are a blur of pure id and emotion in my memory. Perhaps I should not have let those thirty seconds set me adrift. I will admit that is a possible conclusion. The difference between what we brush off our shoulders and what we allow to cut us to the quick is hardly set in stone. Another pastor might have shrugged it off.

I still attended the panel discussion the following day. I may have felt embarrassed, but those who know me will tell you that I am capable of being as stubborn as the most foul-tempered mule. I did not want to slink off with my tail tucked between my legs, chastened by a difficult lesson learned about deigning to ask my elders for alternatives to the church's sacred cows.

The panel consisted of different pastors who gave examples of sermon outlines centered around the stewardship themes that had been explored during the previous day's session. The first pastor got up, and before delving into the guts of her message, pointedly said—and I'm paraphrasing here—"I'll be approaching this particular aspect of stewardship *thematically* because I believe there are multiple ways of preaching this message of Good News."

I looked around the room and saw people smiling and nodding. It was not just me. There was a visible, albeit silent, recognition that there were different and even new ways to preach the same gospel. The radical notion that God speaks in different ways, through different rituals, and via different acts of worship was perhaps not so radical after all—at least in that room.

It remains, I think, still a rather radical notion in the wider institutional church. We in the church have our sacred cows and graven images, whatever they may be, and we cling to the idolatry of what once was, instead of anticipating what might one day be.

Imagine if all we did during, say, Advent, was cling to what once was, instead of anticipating the monumental, life-changing, world-turning-upside-down arrival of the Christ child. Imagine if all we did on Good Friday and Holy Saturday, instead of anticipating the resurrection of the Lord on Easter Sunday, was focus only on the cross. The church would be a hollowed-out shell of what it could be. To many millennial ex-Christians, or millennial Christians on the margins, that is what they see.

But hollowed-out shells can be refilled. New wine can still fill old wineskins, and new wineskins can still be crafted. "They are filled with the new wine," commented the passersby in Acts 2:13 when the Holy Spirit came upon the assembly at nine o'clock in the morning on Pentecost. Better, then, for the church to be filled with such new wine, decanted by the hands and presence of new generations, so that the church may continue to be filled with the Holy Spirit. For it is not as though the church has stopped being attended to by the Spirit; rather, it is that the church's response to such ministrations needs to rise to the mantle of the heritage that Christianity claims: a Messiah who, in dying and rising, gave his followers permission to do the same.

If the choice before the church is to decide whether or not to fear change, then the choice is obvious. We are exhorted to not choose fear at all, whether we raft the river or take the toll road. But for as long as change feels like something to fear, the church will continue to die with no resurrection in sight. I cannot promise that change will stave off death forever, but what I can promise—what the resurrection of Jesus Christ promises—is that death will not have the final word.

In the end, perhaps what most appeals about rafting down a mighty and furious river together is that it leaves another and potentially more optimal way forward for those who will come after us. It represents a different and exhilarating contribution to a well-trod trail. It does not, however, remove the potential of failure. Nothing of this earth can, and nothing of this earth will. Every path, every option, has its own potential pitfalls and obstacles.

But for this endeavor to land upon solid ground, as the pioneers did upon arriving at the Willamette Valley, the church can choose to be what it has not always been: a church for the young as well as for the old; a church for the person of color and the person of LGBTQ identity; a church for the abuse survivor and the homeless person; a church for the differently abled and the mentally ill; a church for the images of God that exist far beyond the faces we typically see in our committees and pulpits.

For as we are about to see, the imperative to be that new church is as urgent as ever.

Chapter 7

It's Not Manifest Destiny
A Church for All

The dim lighting of the restaurant makes it difficult at times to read the full range of emotion on her face. But the anguish in her voice is unmistakable.

"I do not know what is going to happen to me."

"The way they're treating me—my boss, my landlord, my lawyer—it has gotten so terrible."

"I need to stay. They need to know what this means for me."

Over drinks, chicken skewers, and macaroni and cheese, my gaze flickers across the table to a young Yemeni woman my wife is introducing to me. She is sharing the story of her long, drawn-out legal fight for asylum status here in the United States.

I find myself sitting across from a fellow millennial fighting a heroic, bordering on Sisyphean battle against a rising tide of Islamophobia and outright racism alongside seeming indifference from otherwise well-meaning people. I am heartbroken by the chaos and brutality of the xenophobic executive orders issued by the current presidential administration that would have banned her, as a Yemeni, from the country if she were not already living here.

As she recounts her story in a passionate voice that carries a distinct British lilt, I could not help but see in her the century-old image of my great-grandmother, Satenig. She and her husband, my great-grandfather Krikor, fled separately to the United States as refugees during the First World War. On April 24, 1915, the Ottoman Empire rounded up hundreds of Armenians living in the bustling metropolis of Istanbul as the precursor to a genocide that would eventually murder 1.5 million men, women, and children. Within two weeks, my great-great grandfather Sarkis and one of his sons, Krikor's older brother Mardiros, and Mardiros's son, Mourad, were dead. Arrest warrants were issued for Krikor and his remaining brothers, one of whom, Avedis, was arrested and incarcerated. When Ottoman soldiers came to their house demanding to know the rest of the brothers' whereabouts, Mardiros's widow, Esther, told them that the family was long gone. Krikor fled to Vladivostok, Russia, where he met Satenig. From Vladivostok, they sailed to Yokohama, Japan, and then separately across the Pacific Ocean to Seattle (Satenig) and San Francisco (Krikor). They married and eventually settled in the metropolitan area of Detroit, Michigan, where they lived as non-Western immigrants whose second language was English.

My family still has copies of ships' manifests, visas, and Satenig's passport, and those memories counted for something in how my mother and grandmother were raised. During the late 1950s and early 1960s, at the height of the civil rights movement when black Americans were targeted regularly for violence and murders, my mother was in the care of Krikor and Satenig. She remembers my great-grandparents never tolerating a single bigoted or racist comment in their presence. Uttering such prejudices risked a lashing, whether verbal or physical, and neither my mother, nor any of her childhood friends, dared do it.

Krikor and Satenig knew what it meant to be hated for no other reason than simply existing as the "other." Even when politicians were garnering popular acclaim for standing for segregation in the school-house doorways, they brooked no hate in their humble home.

I would not wish what my family experienced on my very worst enemy. But that very experience makes me concerned for American Christianity's present witness—especially white Christianity. If my great-grandparents knew that racism was a losing proposition in the late 1950s, how can we still not have reached such an obvious conclusion in the late 2010s?

We pay the check, and my two dining companions excuse themselves to visit the restroom. Instead of following them out into the brightly lit lobby, I remain a moment longer in my seat, looking down *at my own rough, olive-hued hands. Hands that have spent the past nine years writing sermons and holding people in prayer. Hands that have baptized, married, and buried people. Hands that have painted the church, baked pies, and hidden Easter eggs.*

Hands that, because of the pigment that colors them, are a living, praying reproach to the "America First" agitprop I see playing out all around me today, flying in the face of everything I have come to know about not only my identity, but the Gospel message itself.

Hands that tell me that my work in Christian ministry will never be over, and that the realm of God that I am striving to help build is yet to come.

I reach for my coat and get up from my seat. It is time for these hands to return to work.

The Oregon Trail and Manifest Destiny

The innocuous presentation in the *Oregon Trail* games of American forts and friendly Shoshone tribespeople who would guide you across rivers in exchange for sets of clothing masked a terrible reality. I did not begin to appreciate the sheer scope and scale of that reality until adulthood: the land I set out to claim in a virtual setting was, in reality, taken from another people at the tip of the bayonet, knife, and sword. The expansion of the United States as a nation from the Atlantic Ocean to the Pacific Ocean was the fundamental premise of the doctrine of Manifest Destiny: the United States could, should, and would claim the Wild West because the United States was a peculiar country, special in God's sight, and by God's favor, its growth and expansion were inevitable.

It was one of the costliest doctrines ever conceived, exacting as its price the lives of millions of American Indians over the course of centuries of invasion, conquest, and warfare. The slaughter and forced displacement of American Indians ranks with chattel slavery and Jim Crow laws in the deleterious effects the United States has purposely had upon entire peoples. And like the legacies of slavery and Jim Crow laws, the legacy of the doctrine of Manifest Destiny is still very much alive and with us. It is something that we must face, and offer an accounting for.

Senator Bernie Sanders of Vermont, the darling of many
left-leaning millennials during his upstart bid for the presidency in
2015 and 2016, said in a recent speech to the liberal Jewish lobby,
J Street:

> I think it is very important for everyone, but particularly for pro-
> gressives, to acknowledge the enormous achievement of establish-
> ing a democratic homeland for the Jewish people after centuries
> of displacement and persecution, and particularly after the horror
> of the Holocaust.
>
> But as you all know, there was another side to the story of
> Israel's creation, a more painful side. Like our own country, the
> founding of Israel involved the displacement of hundreds of
> thousands of people already living there, the Palestinian people.
> Over 700,000 people were made refugees.
>
> To acknowledge this painful historical fact does not "dele-
> gitimize" Israel, any more than acknowledging the Trail of Tears
> delegitimizes the United States of America.[1]

Put simply, acknowledging the truth of history does not take away
from also affirming its virtues and existence. It is very much worth
celebrating that a democratic Jewish state exists, and to vigorously
support its existence, just as it is very much worth acknowledging
the human cost at which such a precious homeland came, and advocating for the right of the displaced and occupied Palestinians to
have their own democratic state in the West Bank and Gaza.

Acknowledging historic wrongs does not have to erase an entire
state, or for that matter, an entire church. Narcissa Whitman, one of
the young women whose words I used to open this book, was a missionary with her husband, Marcus, in the Pacific Northwest, where
they were killed in the conflict between white settlers and the Cay-
use tribe, whose homes those settlers were continually encroaching
upon and taking as their own. How they died matters, as does the

---

1. "READ IN FULL: Bernie Sanders' Speech on Israel, Trump, and Anti-Semitism at J
Street Conference," *Haaretz, https://www.haaretz.com/us-news/1.774304*, February 28, 2017,
last accessed December 26, 2017.

context in which they died. The collective memory of atrocities like
the Trail of Tears—the disgraceful episode in which tens of thousands
of American Indians belonging to the Cherokee, Chickasaw, Choctaw,
Muscogee, Ponca, and Seminole tribes were forcibly taken from their
homes, many of them to their deaths—underlines how important
context is. It is of manifold importance for us Americans to acknowledge the harm inflicted by the mentality of "God gave this land to us"
in the name of Manifest Destiny, or the Doctrine of Discovery.

The *Oregon Trail* series glorified aspects of Manifest Destiny and
its underlying Doctrine of Discovery—something that I was oblivious to as a young child playing the video game. As an adult, I am
now profoundly grateful to my denomination for officially rescinding and apologizing for the Doctrine of Discovery in 2017 at our
biannual General Assembly. Even though the revocation and apol-
ogy by itself is not enough, we cannot solve a problem that we pretend does not exist. And we can no longer afford to pretend. What
I fear, along with many millennials (including millennial Christians), is that the election of Donald J. Trump to the presidency will
become one of those historic wrongs that my children, and their
children, will have to acknowledge if there is to be any true salvation
for American Christianity in the future.

Before we discuss the Trump presidency, however, it is crucial to
ask ourselves how we arrived at this administration. As Anthony Hop-
kins, playing another American president—John Quincy Adams—
in the Steven Spielberg film *Amistad* said, "Who we are is who we
were."[2] Who we American Christians have been in the public square
to those outside of the church has often been a face of justifying sin
and intolerance. This has been the millennial generation's experience
of organized Christianity for our entire lives. Beginning with the oust-
ing of President Jimmy Carter in 1980 in response to his administration's removal of tax-exempt status for racially segregated Christian
schools, to the indulgence and enabling of scandal-ridden charlatans
like Peter Popoff and Robert Tilton, to the election of Donald Trump,

2. "Amistad (1997) Quotes," IMDB.com, *https://www.imdb.com/title/ tt0118607/ quotes / ?tab=qt&ref_=tt_trv_qu*, last accessed February 24, 2018.

American Christianity has consistently not practiced what it claimed to be preaching. A reckoning is in order for the Manifest Destiny-esque exceptionalism still claimed by the church.

A Peanut Farmer and Sunday School Teacher

In the original *Oregon Trail* games, one of the three occupations you could pick at the start was a farmer from Illinois, but it was a farmer from Georgia who, because of the moral stands he took, ended up giving us the politically organized Christianity that eventually gave rise to the Trump presidency. Jimmy Carter has been a living, breathing testimony to the profound effect that the Christian faith can have on a soul, and yet, the darling of the nostalgic Christian right is not him, but the man who mobilized the Christian right to vote against him in 1980: Ronald Reagan.

In the 2016 edition of my annual "Ask Me Anything" Christmas thread on Reddit, I was asked about the "Christian = Republican phenomenon." I thought for a minute, and simply said:

> I think that ever since Christians were mobilized to oppose a born-again Sunday school teacher during his presidential re-elect in 1980, many Christians have cared more about being good Republicans first and good Christians second. Put another way: the seeds of that 81 percent of the white evangelical vote breaking for Trump were sown years before I was even born. So, it is going to take a long time to extract that poison from our body.[3]

The mobilization of the church to a particular—often conservative—end is something that millennials were born into. The year 1980 did not mark just the beginning of the birth of the millennial generation as the shift began to swing from Generation X to millennials. It also marked the surprising success of the Reagan Revolution and the solidification of the so-called "Religious Right."

Jimmy Carter remains a widely respected figure in part for how deeply he speaks about his Christian faith. Despite his own personal

---

3. Atcheson, "It's Christmas Eve, and I'm a parish pastor. AMA!"

opposition to abortion—he has said that he never "believed that Jesus Christ would be in favor of abortion"[4]—the fact that the landmark *Roe v. Wade* decision was handed down not during his presidency, but during Richard Nixon's, and his appointing no Supreme Court justices, Carter has become associated with abortion nevertheless. The revisionist histories of the Religious Right paint the movement as a reaction to *Roe* rather than opposition to Carter's enforcement of Nixon's abolition of the federal tax-exempt status for racially segregated religious schools.[5]

Before Carter vs. Reagan came the Nixon vs. Humphrey election in 1968. Nixon's deployment of the so-called "Southern Strategy" fundamentally realigned the nation—not just the South—after thirty-six years of the FDR-influenced New Deal alignment, proving Lyndon Baines Johnson's whispered prophecy in the wake of the landmark Civil Rights Act—"We [Democrats] have lost the South for a generation." By promising a "law-and-order" presidency, Nixon capitalized on white resentment towards the advancement of rights and visibility for people of color in 1968 in much the same way that Trump capitalized upon white resentment towards the visibility of voices and people of color under Barack Obama in 2016.

Thirteen years later, the end of the Carter administration formally marked the ascension of the movement that had been built upon the reaction to Carter. Organizations such as Jerry Falwell's Moral Majority and Ralph Reed's Christian Coalition were dedicated to capitalizing on the newfound mobilization of mostly white Christians as reliable conservative Republican voters. It is difficult to understate the degree to which that political machinery emerged as a response to the Carter White House. Robert P. Jones, the CEO of the Public Religion Research Institute, describes Jerry Falwell's rise to prominence during the Carter years: "[Falwell] became an increasingly vocal critic

---

4. Philip Galanes, "Jimmy Carter and Jacqueline Woodson on Race, Religion, and Rights," *New York Times, https://www.nytimes.com/2015/07/26/fashion/jimmy-carter-and-jacqueline-woodson-on-race-religion-and-rights.html,* July 24, 2015, last accessed December 27, 2017.

5. Randall Ballmer, "The Real Origins of the Christian Right," *Politico, https://www.politico.com/magazine/story/2014/05/religious-right-real-origins-107133,* May 27, 2014, last accessed December 27, 2017.

of the Carter administration. By 1979, he had officially founded the Moral Majority, a political organization that threw its weight behind a Republican rising star: Ronald Reagan."[6]

After Jerry Falwell passed away in 2003, his son Jerry Falwell Jr. carried on the family tradition of hitching its Christian wagon to the coattails of the Republican Party. Falwell Jr. has been one of Donald Trump's most public surrogates, speaking at the Republican National Convention and appearing frequently on television on Trump's behalf. He was rewarded for his loyalty with a mandate to re-examine post-secondary education under the auspices of the Department of Education. As Falwell Jr. and other conservative Christian talking heads like Franklin Graham and Eric Metaxas became visible Trump boosters, the co-option by the Republican Party of the Christian vote that began in 1980 not only continued in 2017, but was amplified. Trump won 81 percent of the white evangelical vote for president, an unprecedented figure in contemporary presidential politics, even as evangelicals of color—who make up roughly 40 percent of the evangelical electorate—largely broke for a United Methodist stalwart in Hillary Clinton.[7]

Trump's candidacy was by no means the first time that Christians have so overwhelmingly responded to so overt a nationalistic message. The church's historical tendency to use nationalism as a dividing point is a very important reason why the United States has a Christian culture that is—at least on paper—disestablished from the federal government. It did, however, represent a culmination of decades of effort to entice today's Christians to do so.

Millennials, then, have literally lived with the Religious Right for our entire lives, and it has played a substantial factor in our generational movement away from organized Christianity. Many millennials came of age in the early 2000s, when same-sex marriage

---

6. Robert P. Jones, *The End of White Christian America* (New York: Simon & Schuster, 2017), 90.

7. Kate Shellnut, "Trump Elected President, Thanks to 4 in 5 White Evangelicals," *Christianity Today*, *http://www.christianitytoday.com/news/2016/november/trump-elected-president-thanks -to-4-in-5-white-evangelicals.html*, November 9, 2016, last accessed December 27, 2017.

bans were passed in dozens of states and the fear of marriage equality was cynically used as a cultural wedge issue to drive so-called "values voters" to the polls. Now, though, nearly seven in ten millennials say the church has driven their peers away by being too judgmental over sexuality.[8] The Faustian bargain struck by conservative Christian voters fifteen years ago is coming due.

Yet only about three in eight seniors feel that the church has in fact been too judgmental over sexuality, a discrepancy of 32 percent, or nearly one in three people.[9] That is a major gap in the understanding of a hugely consequential cultural and political phenomenon, and one that did not go away in the 2016 election despite the coalescing acceptance of marriage equality as the law of the land after Justice Anthony M. Kennedy's landmark decision in the Supreme Court case *Obergefell v. Hodges*. Instead, other culture war relics replaced marriage equality as the wedge issues for Christians.

81 Percent

The 81 percent of white evangelicals who pulled the lever for Donald Trump in 2016 exceeds even the 78 percent of white evangelicals who broke for George W. Bush—a white evangelical who heavily relied on fellow white evangelicals to form his political base—in 2004.[10] Bush, though, is a practicing Christian. Trump, in contrast, professes Christianity and is nominally Presbyterian, but has repeatedly kept the church at arm's length throughout his public life, stating that he has never felt the need to ask for forgiveness and referring to the consecrated host of holy communion as a "little cracker." More than any modern president besides Reagan and

---

8. Amelia Thomson-DeVeaux, "Millennials Leave Their Churches Over Science, Lesbian & Gay Issues," *PRRI*, https://www.prri.org/spotlight/millennials-leave-their-churches-over-science-lesbian-gay-issues/, October 6, 2011, last accessed December 27, 2017.

9. Ibid.

10. Sarah Pulliam Bailey, "White Evangelicals Voted Overwhelmingly for Donald Trump, Exit Polls Show," *Washington Post*, https://www.washingtonpost.com/news/acts-of-faith/wp/2016/11/09/exit-polls-show-white-evangelicals-voted-overwhelmingly-for-donald-trump/?utm_term=.0400dc1b68d5, November 9, 2016, last accessed December 27, 2017.

Bush, Trump has Christian support to thank for his presidency. Yet if only voters under the age of forty had voted, Trump would have lost typically red states like Arizona and Georgia as well as nearly all the swing states that he ended up winning: Florida, Michigan, North Carolina, Ohio, Pennsylvania, and Wisconsin.[11] There was not only a substantial religious divide between Trump voters and Clinton voters, there was a significant generational divide as well.

None of this can fully absolve the millennial generation, and white millennials especially, of Trump's election. Forty-one percent of white millennial voters still cast ballots for Trump, and of those who did, the perception of "white vulnerability" was the biggest common factor in how they voted.[12] It was largely white millennial men who arrayed themselves in Charlottesville to march for white supremacy. And many of the male millennial trolls mentioned in chapter four are also a part of Trump's xenophobic base. Yet that 41 percent need not, and must not, be our generation's voice. Millennials are too diverse a generation to accept such narrow-minded representation, and overall, we did not—we broke for Hillary Clinton by eighteen points.[13]

Much like the Brexit referendum, in which older British voters successfully elected to leave the European Union while Britain's younger voters cast their ballots overwhelmingly to remain in the EU, American millennials live in a world that they did not ask for. Yes, millennial voter turnout remains lower than that of other older generations, especially senior citizens. The phenomenon of older voters being more frequent voters is hardly unique to 2016, but it is slowly changing even as many millennial voters must contend with voter identification laws which specifically omit college IDs as a valid ID

11. Will Drabold, "If Only People under 40 Had Voted, Here's How the Electoral College Would Have Looked," *Mic Network, https://mic.com/articles/159119/if-only-people-under-40-had-voted-here-s-how-the-electoral-college-would-have-looked*, November 10, 2016, last accessed December 27, 2017.

12. Fowler et al., "Why 41 percent of white millennials voted for Trump."

13. William A. Galston and Clara Hendrickson, "How Millennials Voted This Election," Brookings Institute, *https://www.brookings.edu/blog/fixgov/2016/11/21/how-millennials-voted/*, November 21 2016, last accessed February 24, 2018.

with which to vote. It is no exaggeration to say that such laws have been specifically tailored to inhibit a number of demographics from voting: people of color, college students, and millennials.

Banning college IDs in voter ID laws has had an undeniable generational effect. In certain counties in North Carolina, more than half of the early voters who were turned away came from areas with colleges or universities, and while North Carolina's racist gerrymandering laws have since been struck down, recently crafted voter ID laws remain on the books in many states.[14] Texas's notorious voter ID law, which accepted a gun license as a valid form of ID but not a college student ID, was similarly struck down by a federal judge before being reversed 2–1 on appeal.[15] The net effect in the voting booths and the ballot boxes is the same phenomenon that millennials have seen repeatedly in the churches: those with power using it to exclude young voices from the decision-making processes they are entitled to participate in. And in this election, young people were pushed to the sidelines by the 81 percent of white evangelical voters who cast their ballots for Donald Trump as the nation's forty-fifth president.

Rapid Response Mission

On balance, millennials did not want Donald Trump elected president—by a substantial margin—and many of us who did not have resolved to remain vocal in the face of the discord and division that has been sown since. We have reacted to the xenophobia, prejudice, and racism of graffiti, cemetery vandalism, and even arson with acts of charity in donating to the crowdfunding efforts to help repair such damage. Raising awareness through the use of social media is something we touched on in chapter four, but now such outlets are used to draw the attention of friends, family,

14. Lynn Bonner and David Raynor, "Voter ID Law Hinders Some College Students," *Charlotte Observer, http://www.charlotteobserver.com/news/politics-government/ article6570 7922 .html,* March 12, 2016, last accessed December 27, 2017.

15. Josh Gerstein, "Appeals Court, 2-1, Gives Texas OK to Use New Voter ID Law," *Politico, https://www.politico.com/blogs/under-the-radar/2017/09/05/texas-voter-id-law-242352,* September 5, 2017, last accessed December 27, 2017.

and elected officials alike to the hateful actions taking place towards religious and ethnic minority groups.

This is part of how community works for millennials—long gone are the phone trees of old, or even the email chains of, well, less old. Instead, millennials rely on our connections through social media platforms like Facebook and Twitter in order to act as rapid response units, able to inform people of what has taken place and how best to respond to it. The basic function remains the same as the phone trees and email chains: the dissemination of information. But the speed and accessibility at which that information now reaches our ears is unparalleled. This phenomenon has led to a decentralization of the flow of information, and churches that were used to being the focal point of that flow of information have struggled to catch up.

Churches at one time used to be such a hub of activity. You could arrive on a Sunday morning or a Wednesday evening, hear a message or a Bible study touching on an important issue, and be given a set of action steps that you could take after worship was over. Today, no one has to wait until Sunday. People can spring into action the day of an act of vandalism, with thousands of dollars raised for its victims just a day or two later—something my church in Longview experienced in November 2012 when our historic sanctuary building was broken into, vandalized, and nearly set on fire. The rapid response of modern technology made our recovery so much easier. Churches that still cleave to their role as a clearinghouse for not only disseminating information but for discerning possible responses to that information are largely operating out of an outdated mentality towards mission.

Churches can embrace the speed and innovation of social media for their own mission work. Do you have a family in urgent need of funds to stave off eviction? Set aside a line item in your church's weekly or monthly budget, post a link on social media to your church's online giving site, and make it clear that 100 percent of any donations earmarked for the family will go directly to keeping them in their house. Do you urgently need volunteers at a church event or fundraiser for your church preschool? Create a Facebook event, have your friends invite their friends, and generate some buzz all in the span of an afternoon. These are obvious ideas in a generation used to them, but not always obvious in the church. We are increasingly plugged-in creatures, though, and the timeframes for pulling off such feats of coordination are rapidly closing as a result.

In the fall of 2016, right around the time of the election, the Roman Catholic parish across the street from my own congregation was the victim of Nazi-imagery vandalism. Having had our own sanctuary building vandalized and broken into, I felt for them, and I was immediately able to tweet to—and receive a response from—the parish priest letting him know that if there was anything my church could do to help out, we were there for them and were praying for them. It was a relatively small gesture, but one that was still appreciated.

It is a simple way of using social media to do ministry in the face of grotesque acts, but it is an effective way. Through social media, I have seen Muslim veterans offering to stand guard at Jewish cemeteries that were targeted by vandals. I have seen Jewish groups raising donations for burned-down mosques. Such generosity of spirit is what love looks like to me as a Christian minister.

Finally, this means of doing mission has the added benefit of inclusivity because it is not limited only to the people who show up on that Sunday or Wednesday. It is a value that flies in the face of both the quintessentially American mentality of Manifest Destiny and the unmistakable message of American nationalism that we are special rather than inclusive. The millennial generation's response to this mixed legacy of American Christianity, while being widely caricatured as a demand for "safe spaces" for "special snowflakes," is in fact quintessentially Christian, going all the way back to a cantankerous Danish theologian in the 1800s.

The Teleological Suspension

In his landmark work *Fear and Trembling*, the nineteenth-century Danish theologian Soren Kierkegaard wrestles mightily—through his pseudonymous persona Johannes de Silentio—with the story of Abraham's attempted sacrifice of his son Isaac in Genesis 22. Out of his wrestling, Kierkegaard emerges with the belief that "faith is the highest passion in a human being . . . none goes further."[16] While ethical principles—and, indeed, Kierkegaard's own understanding of human ethics—would condemn a father killing his son, Kierkegaard saw in Abraham's actions a belief that faith in God suspended the demands of ethics and made Abraham's attempted murder of his son somehow spiritually acceptable—something that scripture itself says when James cites Abraham's faith as an example in James 2.

Kierkegaard draws a potentially dangerous conclusion. (Just think of all the cult leaders, from Jim Jones to David Koresh, who similarly believed that temporal laws did not apply to them precisely because of how special their faith had to have been.) But turn his thought experiment on its head and ask what we are to do when the government uses ethical means like laws and executive orders to create an immoral ethical body like a federal agency to distribute crime information on illegal immigrants, similar to how Nazi Germany publicized alleged illicit behaviors of German Jews.

What are Christians expected to do in the face of ethical principles promoted by the people of power in our government who dictate that such prejudicial actions are not only lawful, but ethical? What do we do when we are told that it is not only ethical but patriotic to ban an entire religion from our country and to build a wall to blockade an entire race from our borders? Do we go along with a set of ethical principles that is showing its immorality, or do we suspend belief in what our governmental bodies tell us is right in favor of that to which God calls us, even demands of us out of the radical love embodied by Jesus Christ? Are we willing to risk upsetting a system of unjust laws for the sake of social justice?

Does that question seem too extreme an example? Consider the ethical principles that have been constructed within the church over the decades of justifying prosperity theology, financial scandals, and sexual abuse. Those scandals framed the formative years of the millennial generation, and escaping the ethical principles that enabled

---

16. Soren Kierkegaard, *Fear and Trembling*, trans. Alastair Hannay (New York: Penguin Books, 1985), 146.

these scandals constitutes a leap of faith. Even when that leap of faith may not be towards the same interpretation of God, or even towards any God at all, such an exodus from the church indicates there exists a belief in something far greater, beyond what the church has taught millennials can exist. That, too, is a form of faith.

A final word about the image of Abraham about to sacrifice Isaac. When a memorial was commissioned to commemorate the Kent State shootings in 1970 that left four college students dead and another nine wounded for protesting the Vietnam War, the artist, George Segal, elected to fashion a pair of statues—one of Abraham, poised to kill his son, and another of Isaac, bound at his father's feet and begging for his life. The parallels between the bound, younger Isaac and the older, determined Abraham and the young soldiers being drafted to fight and to die at the behest of determined older politicians were so stark that Kent State refused the memorial, saying that it was too controversial. It resides today at Princeton University, by the university chapel.

I wish with all my being that the baby boomers who so passionately protested the Vietnam War, sometimes at the expense of their lives, could once more sympathize with the bound, younger Isaac, about to be sacrificed by older generations. Millennials enlisted in the United States military were sent to fight and to die in two wars in Iraq and Afghanistan. On a broader scale, millennials were sacrificed to the mercilessness of the capitalist economic machine that utterly broke down just as we were entering the job market. At the behest of the economy our elders created, we have sacrificed our livelihoods and our financial security. What we have been left with is each other, which is in no small part why we value inclusivity in both the public and private spheres of our lives.

Honesty with the Past

The millennial need for inclusivity is not limited just to recognizing the present that we are living in, but also the past in all its splendor and sin, wonder and weakness. We crave inclusion not only in our circles of friends and our spiritual communities, but also in the stories that we tell: the stories of our past—our families, our ancestors, and, yes, our country and our church. We tell those stories to one another as well, which is partly why millennials are so apt to see churches and church leaders as hypocrites. We have come of age in an era where organized religion devoted vast sums of both material and spiritual resources to covering up its past. Whether the cover-up was of child abuse, sex scandals, or financial improprieties, in many cases those sins stretched back decades in many churches and denominations. A whitewashing of those sins prevented a true reckoning of the damage done, and destroyed much of the chance for genuine reconciliation with victims and their families. Far from being a place of uplift, affirmation, and growth, the church is too often seen by many of us as a place of manipulation, abuse, and destruction.

In most cases, the sins such scandals centered around were perpetrated by people within the church with access to wealth, influence, or both. They had the capability to shape the narrative and declare their side of the story to be the authoritative one at the expense of their victims, who were silenced rather than believed and not afforded the same platform to tell their story, sometimes for decades. Even today, it remains difficult for victims to speak up out of fear of what detractors may say or do to them.

Until we are honest about those hurtful and shameful parts of the church's past, no matter how painful it is, we will wage a Sisyphean struggle against the understandable and justifiable doubts that my generation holds towards organized religion. Church leaders publicly advocating that the past should stay in the past, without being acknowledged or wrestled with for wisdom, remains a nearly insurmountable obstacle towards recognizing, and reconciling with, those doubts.

Make no mistake: the unwillingness to be honest about the past is in part what has galled many millennials about Donald Trump and his "Make America Great Again" slogan. To us, America was never as great as what we were taught. After all, people of color have had the right to vote for only the past fifty-some years, and as was already noted, that right is again under siege by voter identification laws. Women have had the constitutional right to vote only for the past century. America may indeed have come a long way since the Constitution's composition in 1789, but any country founded upon a document that valued a black slave at three-fifths of a white person will continue to devalue certain people in order to elevate others until new ideals and values are fully brought into being.

During the 2016 election, a short musical video entitled "Make America Great Again" was posted to YouTube by MoveOn.org. It featured two actresses singing about the nostalgic imagery of early- and mid-twentieth-century America, juxtaposed with the social ills of those eras, and in case the target of the video was unclear, it began with an audio clip of Donald Trump promising, "We will make America great again." The song's lyrics include:

> Your husband rarely hit you, and that was ace
>
> Blacks, Jews, and Mexicans knew their place
>
> Back when girls were girls, and men were men
>
> Oh, let's make America great again![17]

None of this is a detail when history textbooks are being ordered by reactionary school boards demanding that the history of Jim Crow laws, slavery, and segregation be minimized, mitigated, or whitewashed. If confession is indeed good for the soul, then a full accounting of what we as American Christians have done to our neighbors, and what we have left undone in helping and aiding them, must be a central part of the church's approach towards millennials, whether or not they are spiritually inclined. Such an accounting is neither easy nor painless. It will take a great deal of self-awareness, honesty, and humility on the church's part. But were the church to do so, it would represent a necessary step forward in the undoing of the damage it has done, both to a generation and to its reputation.

---

17. "LTH Crowd Favorite—Make America Great Again," MoveOn.org, *https://www.you tube.com/watch?v=vf9K5KEs4rE*, September 29, 2016, last accessed December 27, 2017.

Solidarity, Struggle, and Response

This reckoning of ours must be done seriously, lest we see armchair activism as real. You have probably seen the Facebook or Twitter posts, "IF YOU LOVE JESUS, LIKE AND SHARE THIS POST," as though the only begotten Son of God is keeping a personal tally of who likes and shares emotionally manipulative and spiritually vapid posts invoking his name. That cannot be how we share the gospel to new generations of seekers and believers. While I may roll my eyes at the "clicktivism" phenomenon of social media much like a baby boomer, I sincerely hope that I have shown over the last several pages how the millennial generation's engagement with the past, with oppression, and with the need for a truly inclusive world does not hinge solely on liking and sharing things in one another's social media feeds. We are determined to put our money where our mouths (or fingertips) are.

This access to a widespread community matters to millennial Christians in the age of Trump alongside the millennials who have long since jettisoned the church. Devout millennial Christians regularly pop up on my feed lamenting how the same Christian mentors who warned them about the slippery slope of moral relativism have been so enthused by the Trump presidency. The grief in their laments on social media is real and tangible. It is haunting; our equivalent of wailing, or of donning sackcloth and imposing ashes. It is a public display of mourning.

Beyond our mourning, using our social media platforms to provide signal boosts for the causes we care about is our way of showing that we care. It is our version of specialized license plates on our cars, or custom-made return address labels on our mail. We are a generation which acts and votes locally while thinking globally, but we certainly now live and speak globally as well. There are ways in which we as citizens and as Jesus followers can live and speak that global lifestyle and language to reflect our commitment to humane values. None of those ways has to do with age. I genuinely believe that most of us millennials will accept allies who are willing to take our ideas and suggestions seriously, wherever we can find them.

I invite you to be a part of that solidarity. Form a rapid response group to lobby your local leaders on issues of inclusion and diversity as they arise in your area. If anyone in your life is facing down a legal battle over recent executive orders, reach out to immigration lawyers in your area and ask if you can refer them potential clients. Offer to help people in need of an immigration attorney raise money to pay their legal bills. If you are financially able to do so, donate to a church's efforts to aid immigrant families and communities. Most denominations have some sort of structured effort in place to do such important and life-changing mission work. Most importantly, be willing to cede the microphone to someone else when they need to make their voice heard amid the din of noise in the public square.

None of these action steps requires any sort of aptitude for the sorts of digitized communication millennials take as our default means of connecting. But coordinating these steps is greatly helped by such digital media, a lesson that millennials have learned well as the world has grown increasingly smaller to us via our embrace of the current technological revolution.

An embrace of such a global mindset is hardly a sin. Throughout John's Gospel, Jesus moves between Judea, Galilee, and Samaria, with the latter's residents despised by the former's. After short public exchanges, he readily heals members of Canaanite and Roman households just as he does members of Israelite households. He shares water with a Samaritan woman at the well of Jacob. And his disciple Paul's entire career was predicated upon an unshakable willingness to spread the gospel outside the land of Israel to whomever he could.

The New Testament presents an inclusive, not exclusive, Messiah who calls us to struggle and take action together, just as he commissioned the Twelve and then the Seventy, and a global understanding of humanity is a critical part of that. The American exceptionalism that fueled the doctrine of Manifest Destiny is not the message we see in Jesus's public ministry to what he called "the least of these" (Matthew 25:40). Jesus preaches in that passage that what we do to the least of these among us—the oppressed and the marginalized—we likewise do to him. Entire nations, not just a person or group, are judged by God on that basis.

Jesus's ministry has far more to do with what is in our hearts, not what flag we pledge allegiance to. His ministry demands we see in the foreigner and the immigrant the counterpoint to ourselves, and that the factor that most separates us from them is often the genetic lottery that dictated where we were born and whence we came. As a result of Jesus's ministry, we live in solidarity with our fellow soul-vessels who live not only in the United States, but also in Syria, Yemen, South Sudan, and so many other violence-torn places—not because we expect them to follow our beliefs, but because following our beliefs dictates that we live in solidarity with them.

We say no to Manifest Destiny, and its underlying Doctrine of Discovery, because we have seen what it has done, what it has left undone, and we know that God is calling us to something greater than the idols of nationalistic pride and jingoism.

We say no to it because we have come to know that it is borne from an experience and an experiment that must not be repeated, lest similar consequences ensue.

We say no to it because our consciences call us to say no to it, and to do so in ways ranging from our words to our purchases to our choice of religious identity.

In so doing, we say yes to living lives of empathy and solidarity with those whom Jesus champions to us, regardless of their nationality.

Saying No to Manifest Destiny in Action: Charlottesville, Virginia

In the summer of 2017, people descended on Charlottesville, Virginia, to both defend and protest the Confederate statues on the University of Virginia campus. Both sides included large numbers of millennials, but from diametrically opposite moral sides. The statues honored Confederate leaders who fought the United States over one particular vestige of Manifest Destiny: the right of the state to not only legalize, but enable, the forcible enslavement of black flesh. That these statues were even standing in the year 2017 is a sad testament to our love of historical revisionism, and that these statues were so vigorously defended is not just sad, but damning. Hundreds of young men flooded into the college town for their "Unite the Right" event, a barely disguised rally of white supremacy, anti-Semitism, and racism. On the other side of both the street and the spectrum of ideology and morality were groups of counterprotesters, including clergy and college students. Many of them were from older generations, all prepared to speak a much-needed word of truth to the mostly younger white racists who marched on, among other things, a church that was hosting an ecumenical worship service that evening.

One of the challenges millennials face is similar to that of the church—overcoming the horrible image that the millennials of the far-right have plastered all over television and social media. Millennials must learn from just how many people now associate the church with the Caesar-praising, LGBTQ-bashing, Muslim-hating, Trump-kowtowing crowd of those like Jerry Falwell Jr. and Franklin Graham, even though such figures do not represent all of American Christianity. Our generation's association with many odious figures of the modern-day white supremacist "alt-right" movement threatens our own moral fabric and character just as much as Falwell and Graham do for the church.

I pray fervently that the rest of the millennials are beginning to grasp what is at stake. The images that came out of Charlottesville were harrowing, and many of them involved young people putting their bodies in real danger for the sake of standing up to the ideologies of fascism, racism, and Nazism. A small group of UVA students stood at the Thomas Jefferson statue with a sign saying "UVA Students Act Against White Supremacy" as the crowd of hundreds of their fascist age-peers surrounded them with torches. A twenty-year-old black man was beaten to the ground by a group of racists armed with poles. Most tragically of all, thirty-two-year-old Heather Heyer was killed when a twenty-year-old racist drove into a crowd of counterprotesters with his Dodge Charger.

In the aftermath of Heather's murder, other images of her and her life emerged—of her as a child on her father's knee; of her smiling in her professional headshot on the website of the law firm where she worked as a paralegal; and, from Facebook, a picture of her where you can see a small cross sitting on a necklace around her neck.

In the midst of the destruction that white racism produced in Charlottesville, the symbol of Jesus's power over the wages of sin, and the coming future of the empty tomb and its promise of resurrection, was made visible by the person who was martyred for protesting the very worst of ourselves. And when her father, Mark Heyer, was asked about her death, he chose to forgive the domestic terrorist who killed his daughter, citing the words of Jesus on the cross in the Gospel of Luke: "Father, forgive them, for they don't know what they're doing."[18] Enduring what no parent should ever have to endure, a generational elder preached Christ's message to us all.

Testimonies of Heather's compassion and goodness overflowed in media accounts from her family, friends, coworkers, and supervisors. The work of the love that God placed within her was plainly evident, and the hardworking journalists covering her story, as well as the people behind the news outlets' social media accounts on Twitter and Facebook, made sure that her life and story were quickly shared far and wide.

In the face of hatred from radicalized millennials, a millennial woman gave her life, and even more people of goodwill—across all generations—strove to ensure that she would not be forgotten. This sadly was not the first time that such an act—and such a subsequent reaction—had taken place. Only months prior to Heather's death in Charlottesville, another millennial, Taliesin Namkai-Meche, was killed on a MAX train just miles from my home in Portland, Oregon, alongside another hero, Rick Best. They were defending two young girls of color, one of them Muslim, from a white racist who then murdered the two men.

---

18. "WATCH: Father Talks about Daughter Killed at Charlottesville Protest," *Asbury Park Press, https://twitter.com/AsburyParkPress/status/897269112354648068*, August 14, 2017, last accessed December 27, 2017.

There is no resurrection that brings someone killed by white supremacy back from the dead, except in the way Christ's own resurrection meant that the false supremacy of the Romans who had beaten and crucified him would not be the final word. The love of God as expressed by the humanity who chooses to follow the ways of God is the final word. There is life in that, and for that reason alone, my generation—and the church across all generations, including future ones—should see a role for ourselves in resisting the prejudices and bigotries that are having their moment in the sun.

Responding with resurrection to the hatred and death that racism promises can be the template for the church and millennials alike. Putting resurrection into action by honoring the pain and loss we experience and heeding what our elders have to teach us about such pain can offer my generation a way forward in putting its spiritual imprint on a world that remains broken and crying out for healing.

That promise of resurrection should also be a lesson especially for those in my generation who have aligned themselves with the anti-Christ ideologies of fascism, Nazism, and white racism. The rest of our generation far exceed you, not merely in numbers but also in justness and righteousness. You may have your moment in the spotlight, but the rest of us will retain our consciences. And those consciences that you so sorely lack will be what God ultimately uses to build a world that quashes with divine love and justice the small-minded, hard-hearted agitprop to which you subscribe.

A Guest Room Sits Empty, for Now

I arrived home from the restaurant where my wife and I had enjoyed dinner with the young Yemeni woman who had been pouring out her story to us. As I do each time I arrive home, I slid off my shoes by the closet and opened its door to put my winter coat away.

Then I turned and looked across our front hallway to the spare bedroom that sits behind our garage. When my wife and I bought our home a couple of years ago, we intended for this spare room to be our guest room. Because it has a full bathroom and connects to the rest of the house only through that narrow hallway, it affords much more privacy than our second bedroom upstairs, and we have friends and family who appreciate that.

We have had many of those friends and family visit us on and off and stay in that room ever since we moved in, but at that moment, the guest room sat empty.

I do not know for how much longer.

Our Yemeni friend deliberated a move to Canada because of the xenophobia emboldened by the current president. But Yemen is on the list of countries in the president's travel ban. She would not be able to return to the United States if she left. So Carrie and I decided together that if our friend remains in the United States and Immigration and Customs Enforcement begins doing extensive sweeps in Portland, or issues a deportation order for her, we would invite her to stay with us until she could safely return home. Our empty guest room may end up a sanctuary.

We realize that our aiding someone without in-order papers to remain in the country will be looked down upon by some, perhaps by many, as us actively flouting the rule of law. But they do not know my story, or the stories my generation carries with us. Young though we are, we millennials carry with us the stories and values of our elders. I was in the room when, at the 2017 General Assembly of my denomination, the Christian Church (Disciples of Christ), it was the older Disciples pastor and prophet William J. Barber II who brought the whole assembly to its feet with shouts of approval when he bellowed, not at a worship service or a protest, but at a business meeting of all contexts, "They cannot arrest us all! Let ICE arrest us at our communion tables!" The moral voice of one of our elders spoke to us, and we roared our respect and appreciation.

We treasure these stories and values. We cherish them. And we fiercely guard them. As long as there is breath in my body, I will continue telling the story of how my courageous great-grandparents, when they were both younger than I am now, successfully smuggled themselves out of a genocide. I will continue telling the story of how they transported themselves out of desperation to a land where they could be safe and have a family and live lives that did honor and justice to the loved ones they left behind in the dust of Anatolia. I will continue telling that story not only because it is my birthright, but because it is an integral part of my own spiritual liberation.

We millennials share these stories and their morals, whether we are descended from slaves, refugees, workers, immigrants, or indigenous people. We are storytellers. We post our stories on our platforms, our blogs and our social media pages. We point others towards them. We write our stories and we share them. Sometimes, our stories become testimonies that move us to action against those with the power to determine the future of those whose stories we tell. These stories become testaments to both who we are and *whose* we are, to our identities as people and to our identities as children of—and creatures of—the one God of all.

The treatment of the marginalized, the oppressed, and the downtrodden needs to be a "Here we stand; we can do no other" moment for not only millennials, but the entire church. The current state of unwelcome in which we live demands radical, countercultural resistance from us. Many in my generation feel compelled to act, perhaps differently than other generations might, and certainly to vote differently, but to act and vote nonetheless, and to do so with urgency and vigor.

And if our choosing mercy and inclusion over the harshness of our Caesar's law somehow merits negative judgment, I know that God is merciful, and I know that God will have mercy upon us.

For it is a great praise of God to say that God is merciful, that God is welcoming, and that God is inclusive. And it is right that we should give God such praise. In fact, it is where we get the word "hallelujah" from—it literally means to praise God or to praise God to the people.

Let that divine capacity for mercy be my parting hallelujah, my praise of God, to you.

Journeying the Trail Again

"I could not realize that the end of our long journey was so near."

"I did not think it would take us this long to search for a new home and family."

"We have not found a place that really feels like home yet. We hope our search ends here."

The first of these three sentiments comes once again from the twenty-eight-year-old missionary Narcissa Whitman, who traveled the Oregon Trail westward with her husband, Marcus, in 1836.[1] The other two sentiments again represent the sort of refrains I hear frequently from seekers in search of a spiritual community. Much as it struck Narcissa Whitman with happy disbelief that her long journey was nearing its end, so too did I see the similarly joyful disbelief from pilgrims who passed through the stately double doors of the historic church I pastored for nearly seven years in the heart of Longview, Washington. They hoped that their own winding journey in search of a spiritual home had at long last reached its end. And for many of them, it did.

These new souls I received in my role as a pastor of a small-town congregation shared in many of the tentative but deep-seated desires that I, and so many other millennial Christians, possess: to grow in faith surrounded by people who accept us for who we are and who God made us to be—not for who the church wants us to become for its own shortsighted reasons.

The level of acceptance makes all the difference. While we should challenge people to change, transform, and evolve as a part of

---

1. "Narcissa Whitman," National Park Service.

a spiritual community, demanding such change overnight is unfair, especially from an organization that has been notoriously reluctant to change its own ways. Before any life-changing metamorphosis can take place for most people in their spiritual community, an honest accounting of that person's past experiences is a prerequisite. I cannot expect someone to follow me, as a pastor, towards God without honoring their past experiences with clergy who may have spiritually manipulated, misled, or abused them. Nor can I expect someone to become a member of a congregation that I pastor without my honoring their past experiences with congregations that may have mistreated, bullied, or even exiled them.

Nor should we expect the same of millennials—or any generation, for that matter—who make the courageous decision to begin a new journey within the folds of church life once more. Churches cannot expect millennials to move faster to begin their new journeys than churches are themselves willing to move. Yet that is what the church often expects of its young visitors, who return seeking membership only to retreat once more when they are left alone on the outside of the circled-up wagons.

Starting a new game of *Oregon Trail* is as simple as coming up with some new nicknames for your fictitious family members. As soon as you arrive in the Willamette Valley and enter your name into the high score list, you can start journeying the Oregon Trail all over again. But starting a journey of faith and spiritual searching over after someone has felt left on the outside looking in by the institutional church is often a far more intimidating proposition. One negative experience with a parish or a pastor can be the impetus for retreating from organized religion, and understandably so. The act of retreating, in turn, can bring the act of restarting the journey to a full stop. Instead of striking out on a journey they may have begun years ago at a parent's knee in church, many millennials have remained forever at the edge of the river, looking out at the other side, without the incentive to cross the tumultuous waters.

Over the past seven chapters, I hope I have laid out a clear path across those boundaries that separate my generation from other

generations of Christians. I have not tried to be the voice of a generation, but I have tried to be one voice for the part of it that has not
yet given up on Christianity and its teachings.

It is impossible to be a voice for my generation, as diverse and
inundated with information and opinions as we are. Please do not
take my words or experiences as universal. But there are common
cultural bonds that we share as millennials that I have tried to share
here, and that I hope you in turn will share with others seeking
to better understand, reach out to, and minister to this amazing
generation.

While portions of this book were written at my boyhood home
outside of Kansas City, where my parents still reside, most of it was
penned in the living room of the modest townhouse in southwest
Washington state that my wife and I call home, an hour or so from
the lush greenery of the Willamette Valley and the end of the historic Oregon Trail. I have made my home here, such as it is. This is
a home that fits, that feels good and right, and is exactly what I need
it to be right now.

That is what millennials are searching for, craving, and asking for from both their spiritual and physical homes. The need
for deep acceptance means that we will continue traveling, living,
and searching around the periphery of the church, or outside of it
altogether, before entering into the goodness and greatness that the
church can be.

For millennials to begin that journey into the church once
again, we have to believe that the benefits are worth the inherent
risk in making ourselves vulnerable to an institution that has circled its wagons, seeing any outsiders as potential threats, and that
has preyed on peoples' vulnerabilities rather than cherished them.
Circling up the wagons keeps the wagon train from moving forward
together on the trail in its quest for a new home.

Our youngest generation, Generation Z, has begun its own
journey fast behind the millennial generation. In its ministry to
Generation Z, the church would do well to avoid the pitfalls in its
relationship with millennials. Recommitting to becoming a church

that preaches words of welcome to the young is not enough; the church must also purposefully welcome them and demand deliberation, sacrifice, and substantive changes in how it decides to minister to younger generations. The lessons the church is learning with its millennial cohort will serve it well as it rededicates itself to reaching out to still younger generations.

Being church for every new generation is not as easy as beginning a new game of *Oregon Trail*, but it is far more consequential and rewarding. It is also far more important.

This is the work that lies ahead of the Church as we reboot and recalibrate our spiritual selves, and our spiritual communities, for this long-awaited generation of seekers. And what holy work it is!

I pray for God's blessing upon you as you discern your own route forward along the trail, wherever that route may take you, so long as it brings you ever closer to the One who created you, who redeemed you, and who sustains you.

Vancouver, Washington
February 2018